EXPLORING
THE FAR NORTH WEST OF SCOTLAND

A walker's guide to the hills, glens and coastline
of Wester Ross and Sutherland

RICHARD GILBERT

EXPLORING
THE FAR NORTH WEST OF SCOTLAND

A walker's guide to the hills, glens and coastline
of Wester Ross and Sutherland

CORDEE – LEICESTER

Copyright © 2000 by Richard Gilbert

First published 1994 by Cordee Ltd, Leicester
Fully revised 2000

Trade enquiries to Cordee Ltd,
3a De Montfort Street, Leicester LE1 7HD
www.cordee.co.uk

**British Library Cataloguing in
Publication Data**
A catalogue record for this book is available
from the British Library

ISBN 1 871890 27 6

Front cover: Beinn Alligin and Loch Torridon seen
from the west ridge of Mullach an Rathain on
Liathach. Photo: Richard Gilbert.

Frontispiece: Canisp and Suilven tower over the
picturesque white fish port of Lochinver in
Sutherland. Photo: Ian Wild.

Rear cover: Slioch seen from the woods of
Caledonian pine on the south side of Loch Maree.
Photo: Ian Evans.

**Photoset by Parker Typesetting Service,
Leicester**

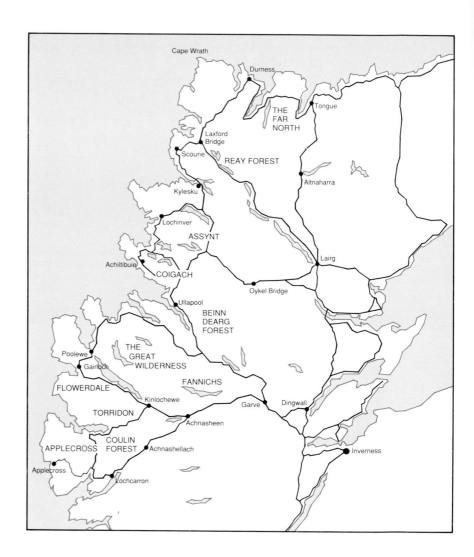

CONTENTS

ACKNOWLEDGEMENTS

This book has been in preparation for a long time and I am deeply grateful for the help of many people. For companionship on the hills I am indebted to my wife Trisha, my children Timothy, Emily, Lucy and William and also many friends, in particular Gerard Simpson and Paul Hawksworth.

The production of the book has been in the capable hands of my publisher, Ken Vickers, editor Heather MacDermid, and Ivan Cumberpatch has devoted much time and skill in the preparation of the maps. Pat Leigh has patiently typed numerous drafts of the script.

The photographs printed were selected from a total of 3,500 which were submitted by friends and acquaintances, for which I am extremely grateful. In particular I must mention Stuart Bramwell, Iain Brown, Ken Bryan, Irvine Butterfield, Steve Chadwick, Phil Cooper, Ian Evans, Gordon Gadsby, Richard Gibbens, Lucy Gilbert, Stephen Greenwood, Alan O'Brien, Tom Rix, Ian Wild. The prolific photographer Jim Teesdale made many visits to the hills to fill specific gaps.

Richard Gilbert has been an active mountaineer and hill walker for over forty-five years. He is an ex-president of the Oxford University Mountaineering Club and is a member of the Climbers Club and the Alpine Club.

He has climbed in many countries in the world but his greatest love is the Scottish Highlands. He was the 101st Munroist in 1971 and soon after bought a house in Wester Ross where he and his family spend much of their spare time.

For nearly thirty years he has taught chemistry at Ampleforth College in North Yorkshire where he founded a flourishing mountaineering and expeditions club. In 1977 he was made a Winston Churchill Fellow for leading the first-ever school expedition to the Himalayas.

Other books by the author:

Hill Walking In Scotland, Thornhill Press.
Young Explorers, G. H. Smith.
Mountaineerig For All, Batsford.
Memorable Munros, Diadem.
The Big Walks (with Ken Wilson), Diadem.
Classic Walks (with Ken Wilson), Diadem.
Wild Walks (with Ken Wilson), Diadem.
200 Challenging Walks, Diadem.
Lonely Hills and Wilderness Trails, David and Charles.

PREFACE

This is a guidebook to the most beautiful, rugged and undiscovered corner of Britain. It caters for hardened mountaineers looking for severe challenges in the hills, for modest walkers who seek worthwhile objectives to explore and for visitors and families who seek peace, tranquillity and relaxation amongst the lochs, glens, hills and sandy bays of this unique area.

From Kyle of Lochalsh to Cape Wrath the Atlantic Ocean pounds the coast of Wester Ross and Sutherland. Tiny coves, broad strands, shingle beaches, broken cliffs, blow holes, sea stacks, islets and skerries have been carved out by the restless waves over many thousands of years.

Inland, beyond the dunes, marram grass and machair, rise some of the steepest and most individual mountains to be found anywhere in Europe. Sea lochs penetrate deeply into the mountain ranges providing a unique and glorious combination of grandeur and remoteness. To sit beside the summit cairn on a west coast peak and gaze out across the Minch to the hills of Harris silhouetted against a fiery sky, is to get close to paradise.

This guidebook covers the area of Wester Ross and Sutherland north of the Garve to Kyle of Lochalsh railway line, while the eastern boundary passes through Strathvaich and Strathcarron to Lairg and then follows the line of the A836 to Tongue. Administratively the whole area is within Highland Region.

I have covered all the principal mountains in this area irrespective of height for, in the North West Highlands, the status of Munro (separate mountain over 3000ft) or Corbett (separate mountain between 2500ft and 3000ft with a drop of at least 500ft on all sides) is not an important criterion. Such gems as Ben Stack, Suilven, Stac Pollaidh, Ben Mor Coigach, Beinn Ghobhlach and Beinn a'Chearcaill do not make either list yet can be guaranteed to provide memorable days for the connoisseur.

I have climbed old favourites such as An Teallach well over a dozen times and the pleasure never fades. Even the less fashionable Corbetts, several of which I climbed only recently for the purpose of including them in this book, gave me wonderful mountain days with visits to hitherto unknown corries, gorges and glens and unusual prospects of better known peaks. For the record, ascents of all the thirty-five Munros and thirty-nine Corbetts within the area are described.

But the North West Highlands have much more to offer than just climbing mountains. I have therefore described many walks that traverse mountain ranges keeping to the lower ground. Coastal walks too get a separate chapter, for the sea's constant ebb and flow, accompanied by the suck and roar of the breakers, is akin to the moaning of the wind and the erosion by rain and frost of mountain peaks. In both cases we see the forces of nature at work.

I defy any walker not to be enthralled by his or her first view of the white combers racing across the mile-wide stretch of sand at Sandwood Bay, by the thousands of auks contesting nest sites on the Stack of Handa during the breeding season, by the fragrant aroma of sea pinks on the cliffs at Reiff in June or by the frightening ferocity of the waves crashing against the Point of Stoer during a winter storm with seals playing in the boiling surf.

Every visitor to the region will need a few relaxing days away from the mountains, glens and coastline. The weather may not

Liathach, one of the giants of Wester Ross, is seen in this classic view across Loch Bharranch in Glen Torridon. Photo: Ian Evans.

always be friendly and so I have included an extended chapter on places of interest, historic sites, houses and gardens, waterfalls and caves which are open to the public and can make modest objectives or can be explored.

I have tried to cater for the needs of families with young children by listing the principal sandy bays and beaches all the way up the coast from Kyle of Lochalsh to Cape Wrath. It cannot be assumed however, that bathing is safe at all the bays listed; steeply shelving beaches, currents and a strong undertow are common dangers. Local information should be sought and bathers should remember that there will be no life guards on duty.

Accommodation should not be a problem, even in the height of the holiday season. In addition to hotels and guesthouses a large number of private houses offer bed and breakfast in the summer months. The local Tourist Information Centres hold complete lists of available accommodation and will, for a small fee, book ahead to meet your requirements. Full details of caravan parks and camp sites as well as local events and attractions can also be found at the Information Centres, a list of which, together with phone numbers, is given in the appendix.

Structure and Landscape

The special qualities of the North West Highlands are due to many factors of which the most important is the extremely complex geological structure.

Scotland's western seaboard was once the shore and delta of an ancient continent, one of the first land masses in the world. In general the base rock is Lewisian gneiss, a hard crystalline and exceptionally ancient rock formed over 2,000 million years ago. Lewisian gneiss is responsible for the myriad lochans which fill every scoop and hollow in the Scourie-Rhiconich area and it rises to 3000 ft on Ross-shire's A'Mhaighdean.

Yet throughout much of the north-west the gneiss has been overlaid by red Torridonian sandstone which was formed in warm, shallow seas about 1,000 million years ago and in places was 2000ft thick.

The third main series of geological formations was a further overlaying process of Cambrian quartzite. This startlingly white-grey rock can be seen in spectacular fashion on hills such as Beinn Eighe, Foinaven and the north side of An Teallach. The hard quartzite layer has protected the underlying sandstone from severe weathering but hills without this protection have eroded severely. Good examples are the stark, isolated monoliths of Stac Pollaidh and Suilven, which is to many people the most impressive hill in all Scotland.

The Cambrian era also saw the deposition of Durness limestone which has resulted in oases of greenery and some spectacular cave systems, particularly in the areas of Inchnadamph and Durness.

A further important influence on the geology of the northwest was the Moine thrust which occurred about 430 million years ago. Heaving of the earth's crust moved vast areas of metamorphic rock in a north-westerly direction, forcing it over and above more recent rock such as limestone. This tangle of seemingly contradictory evidence was first unravelled by Professor Nicol in an historic paper published in 1859.

Much more recently a succession of ice ages and their accompanying glaciers gouged out corries, hanging valleys, deep glens and sea lochs leaving mounds of moraine and erratics which have been carried many miles from their original mountains.

When the ice finally departed, about 10,000 years ago, the earth's crust, relieved of the weight, lifted to give raised beaches which are very prominent beside Loch Carron and Loch Torridon. The climate became warmer and vegetation spread: Scots pine, oak, holly, hazel, birch, aspen and rowan grow on the lower ground with alder and willow along the rivers.

Although humans have destroyed much of the tree cover of the Highlands by burning, felling and over grazing some prime examples still remain. The area around Loch Maree is one of the best for remnant woodlands with oak woods on the north shores and splendidly gnarled Scots pines and other species on the south side. This latter area is now part of the Beinn Eighe National Nature Reserve and receives careful attention. Nevertheless, the original extent of the old forest is brought home to the walker who battles with peat bogs and hags, for bleached roots of ancient pines are often visible when they protrude from beneath the turf.

The dead hand of regimented forestry with foreign species has, thankfully, not been developed to any great extent in the far north-west. Certainly there are many commercial forestry projects but there is not the blanket afforestation with conifers which is all too obvious in the Southern Uplands, the Grampians and the Flow Country of eastern Sutherland and Caithness.

The very remoteness of north-west Scotland has lessened the visitor pressure for caravan sites, building plots, access roads, picnic sites and car parks and this has helped to preserve its wilderness aura. Estates tend to be very large and the land-owners have resisted intrusive developments, preferring to rely on income from the traditional sources of deer stalking and fishing. For these reasons the vast tract of wild mountainous country between Loch Maree and Little Loch Broom is still a magnificently primeval region which has come to be known as *The Great Wilderness*.

Weather

My final point about the appeal of the North West Highlands concerns the weather. Far too many people who have little or no experience of the area throw up their hands in horror at the mention of north-west Scotland. 'Oh, but it rains all the time,' they exclaim. The facts are somewhat different.

Cape Wrath has an annual rainfall approximately equal to that of Penzance and considerably less than Windermere. Apple-cross, further south, equates roughly with Keswick and is very much drier than Fort William. May and June are the best months for sunshine in Wester Ross and Sutherland.

In this far corner of Britain the weather is often changeable with a brisk wind scudding the clouds across the sky, but this can produce a day of contrasts with an exceptional quality of light and an exhilarating sharpness in the air.

The mountains tend to make their own weather and forecasts can be unrealiable. It is even worth setting off in rain, for

changes can be sudden and dramatic. Clouds can roll away to reveal black, dripping crags, wreaths of mist in the gullies, rainbows and tumbling burns. If you are lucky you may climb above the cloud into a fairytale world where just the tops of the highest mountains appear above a sea of cotton wool and the sun beams down from a cloudless sky.

Safety Notes

Many of the walks in this book are far from help and several are major mountaineering routes. The weather is fickle and only a few of the low level routes are waymarked. Thus it is essential to take proper safety precautions.

Inexperienced walkers should work gradually through some of the shorter, easier expeditions before embarking on the high, serious mountain traverses. You will soon be able to compare your times with mine and so make the necessary adjustments. (Note that my estimated times are for fit walkers and do not include stops.)

Efficient and accurate map and compass work must become second nature. Keep your map and compass in your anorak pocket and refer to them regularly, for at all times you should know exactly where you are in the hills. It is sensible to study the map and guidebook and to note important bearings before leaving the shelter of the valley, not on an exposed ridge in a rainstorm.

In the mountains situations can change rapidly, requiring bold decisions. In the face of threatening weather, approaching darkness or the tiring of a member of the party it is essential to get off the high ground and into the valley by the quickest possible route. If in doubt, don't forge on hoping for the best; turn round and return to base.

I would never advocate carrying heavy rucksacks packed with safety gear to cope with every possible eventuality, but certain items are essential. The main priorities are warm clothes, efficient waterproofs and, in winter, ice-axe and crampons. Emergency food, whistle, map, compass, first-aid kit, torch and exposure bag should be packed as a matter of course.

Hard snow lingers well into early summer on north-facing slopes and corries and ice-axes should be taken if there is even a remote possibility of meeting snow. If you do meet snow don't leave your ice-axe strapped to the back of your rucksack but have it in your hand.

Many routes involve river crossings. I have indicated the most notorious crossings in the text but even the mildest burn can become a raging torrent in times of flood. A light-weight safety rope should be carried if you are in any doubt about the route or the conditions. Drowning accidents are by no means uncommon in the Highlands.

If you leave your car parked in a mountain area, leave a note behind the windscreen giving your name, route and estimated time of return. If you are staying at a Youth Hostel or hotel, leave details of your proposed itinerary with someone in authority.

If an accident should occur, you must carry out the emergency drill:

    a) The International Distress Call is six blasts on a whistle, or six shouts or flashes of a torch. The answering signal is three blasts.

    b) After first fixing a map reference for the position of the casualty, send a fit member of the party to summon help. He/she should dial 999 and report to the Police, who co-ordinate all mountain rescue services.

Responsibility

Many mountain areas in Britain are suffering from erosion from the sheer number of boots that trample them. While Wester Ross and Sutherland do not yet suffer too badly from erosion I do hope that readers of this guide will be alert to the problem and do their best to minimise their impact.

Walkers should wear the lightest footwear appropriate to the conditions. While heavy boots may be necessary for many of the rocky ridges and boulder strewn slopes they are not necessary for most low level and coastal walks. Not only are heavy boots tiring to wear but they cause damage to the structure of the peat, damage which leads to poor drainage, water-logged ground and erosion. If you can step on rocks rather than turf you should always do so, for rocks can withstand wear and tear whereas vegetation has but a precarious hold on the thin top-soil of the mountains. Likewise if you are using a path which zig-zags up a hillside don't show off your fitness by cutting off the corners. You will only cause an ugly scar and hasten erosion.

May I also appeal to walkers not to build new cairns or add stones to existing ones? Our mountains are now over-cairned and this detracts from the aura of wilderness.

Metric Matters

At the time of writing we are in slow transition from the long-standing British linear measurements of miles, yards and feet to their metric equivalents.

All the new maps are now using metres for spot heights but walkers, perhaps mindful of the Munro and Corbett classifications, still tend to feel easier with the old system.

In this guide I have, where appropriate, used both systems for length and height realising that, like the Fahrenheit and Celsius temperature measurements, the transition to metres and kilometres will take a very long time.

Walkers with the old one inch O.S. maps, which record height in feet, may be puzzled by the new spot heights that I have given. Since the most recent survey of the hills was recorded in metres I have used the multiplication factor of 3.281 to obtain the most accurate equivalent in feet.

Access

The described walks do not necessarily follow designated rights-of-way, although not once have I ever been challenged in Wester Ross or Sutherland. The traditional 'right-to-roam' is thankfully being acknowledged by the landowners, and so it is most important to preserve goodwill by:

    a) Courteous co-operation with farmers and landowners.

    b) Scrupulous adherence to the Country Code.

    c) Never climbing dry stone walls or deer fences. (Always look for gates.)

d) Checking locally before going onto the hills during the deer stalking season (roughly mid-August to mid-October).
e) Keeping dogs under strict control and on a lead in the vicinity of farms and areas of grazing.

It is over thirty years since my first visit to the Far North West and over twenty years since my wife and I established a base in Wester Ross. The majority of our holidays have been spent exploring the area and our four children have been brought up to enjoy camping at Sandwood Bay and on the Summer Isles, barbecues at Gruinard, bird watching at Handa and scrambling over the mountain crests at all seasons. I hope that this book will enable others to fully enjoy this unique area of Scotland which has so much to offer the adventurous visitor.

The guide provides lots of information and ideas but it does not claim to cover every hill, corrie and glen in Wester Ross and Sutherland; the satisfaction of more detailed exploration is left to the reader.

I have personally visited every bay and walked every route described in this book, the more popular itineraries many times, but changes do occur and I apologise in advance for any errors and discrepancies.

RICHARD GILBERT
Ullapool
Wester Ross 1994

In early summer sea pinks bloom on the cliffs of Handa Island, an RSPB bird reserve off the Sutherland coast. Photo: Alan O'Brien.

1 APPLECROSS

The Applecross peninsula is a unique area of the North West Highlands characterised by a major group of steep sandstone mountains, numerous corries, a high desolate plateau and an exquisitely wild and rugged coastline. A notoriously steep motor road, gradient 1 in 3, crosses the mountains at the Bealach na Ba before descending to the tiny settlement of Applecross village. For many years this road, which is the second highest in Britain, provided the only access to Applecross but nowadays you can drive north through the crofting communities at Fearnbeg and Kenmore to meet the A896 at Shieldaig.

There are several Norse place names on Applecross, such as Toscaig, resulting from the Norse rule of the Hebrides for nearly 400 years from the ninth century.

But it is the wonderful mountains of Applecross that provide the best walks on the peninsula. They sit squatly on the barren moors west of Glen Shieldaig and, when seen from the high road between Lochcarron and Kishorn or from Beinn Damh, they resemble freshly baked loaves, removed from the oven and set out in a line to cool. In the early morning, sunshine floods into the corries of Beinn Bhan and Sgurr a'Chaorachain highlighting their magnificent rock architecture.

The main hill south of the Bealach na Ba, Meall Gorm, is only a few minutes walk away from the layby at the top of the road and this needs no detailed description. I have therefore restricted my account of the Applecross hills to the two main tops, Beinn Bhan and Sgurr a'Chaorachain, which can be taken together or split into two shorter expeditions by using the splendidly wild Coire nan Arr as a means of approach or return.

On Beinn Bhan in the Applecross Hills. A series of east-facing corries bite deeply into the summit plateau. Photo: Gordon Gadsby.

Beinn Bhan 2939ft/896m and Sgurr a'Chaorachain 2599ft/792m

> *Start/Finish:* Tornapress (838422)
> *Map:* O.S. 1:50,000 Sheet 24
> *Distance:* 13 miles, 21km
> *Time:* 7–8 hours
> *Grading:* A long day amidst rugged and rocky mountains. Difficult route finding in mist. The walk can be cut short easily if required.

Even by Torridon standards the corries and buttresses of the Applecross Hills are impressive, with miles of cliffs and acres of steep, bare rock. On the north side Beinn Bhan sends down four great corries ringed by cliffs. Proceeding south, the wide Coire nan Arr penetrates deeply into the hills dividing Beinn Bhan from Sgurr a'Chaorachain, whose mighty eastern spur towers above the now derelict Howard Doris construction yard on the shores of Loch Kishorn.

Fascinating and awe-inspiring, this walk runs under the corries of Beinn Bhan, climbs the rocky ridge to the northern summit of the mountain, traverses round the cliff-edge of Coire nan Arr to Sgurr a'Chaorachain and then descends the terraced nose to the road. There is no path and it calls for some scrambling and route-finding ability and a good head for heights, and so I have included some easier alternatives for the less confident.

Park near the bridge at Tornapress, take the Loch Gaineamhach path for a mile and then make a rising traverse to Lochan Coire na Poite. This is a lonely and picturesque lochan set in a wild amphitheatre. A buttress of rock rises dizzily for 1000ft

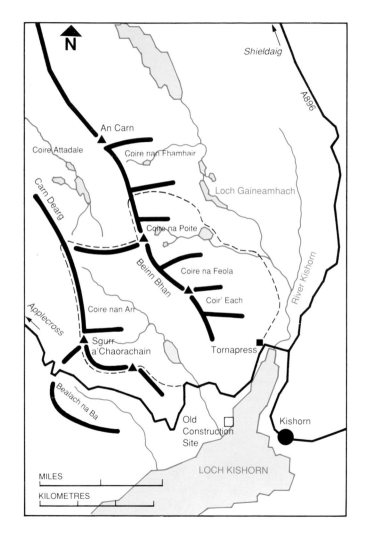

into the main corrie, while a natural rock dam forms an inner corrie enclosing two more lochans.

A broad ridge of broken sandstone outcrops runs out from the north side of the corrie and this provides an entertaining scrambly route of ascent to the summit plateau of Beinn Bhan. Alternatively, contour round into the next corrie, Coire nan Fhamhair, and find an easier way to the plateau.

Surprisingly, you meet a shallow lochan surrounded by lush grass on Beinn Bhan. Hug the edge of the cliffs to give yourself sensational views down plunging precipices into the heart of Coire na Poite, as well as west to Dun Caan on Raasay and the Quirang on Skye.

From Beinn Bhan's summit it is a long and rough descent over shattered boulders to Bealach nan Arr and subsequent ascent to the radio mast on Sgurr a'Chaorachain. If you wish to cut the walk short an easy escape route is down Coire nan Arr to the road near the bridge over the Russel Burn.

Coire nan Arr also provides a pleasant way up Sgurr a'Chaorachain if this mountain is to be climbed as the sole objective on a day's walk.

The radio mast is a hideous intrusion into such a magnificent mountain environment and you should hurry past it along the quite narrow east ridge to gain the principal summit of Sgurr a'Chaorachain. The ridge provides a close view of the prodigious Cioch buttress which juts out into Coire nan Arr like the prow of an ocean liner. The direct ascent of the Cioch nose is a classic rock climb of 1300ft 400m at Very Difficult standard giving some remarkably exposed pitches.

Experienced mountaineers can negotiate the very steep, terraced abutment of Sgurr a'Chaorachain to descend directly towards Tornapress. Others must return to the radio mast and descend easy slopes to Bealach na Ba.

Left: A'Cioch of Sgurr a'Chaorachain, a buttress of Torridonian sandstone rising abruptly above Loch Coire nan Arr in the Applecross Hills. Photo: Iain Brown.

Right: Looking south over the cliffs of Meall Gorm to Loch Carron from Sgurr a'Chaorachain in the Applecross Hills. Photo: Jim Teesdale.

2 THE BEN-DAMPH AND COULIN FORESTS

Exploration of the Ben-Damph and Coulin Forest areas gives the best possible introduction to the North West Highlands. Within this area there is a high concentration of steep rock peaks which rise abruptly from the corrie floor, a characteristic that is typical of much of Wester Ross and Sutherland.

The extraordinary mountain formations were caused by the Moine thrust dislocation, when enormous lateral pressures produced geological chaos and confusion. In many places older Torridonian sandstone was thrust upwards over newer Cambrian quartzite causing a unique sandwich. Much later came weathering and glaciation which caused further changes of form.

Many of the corries are boggy with cotton grass and bog asphodel growing in profusion. The better drained upper slopes support juniper and are bright with tormentil, sea pinks (thrift) and thyme.

A splendid network of stalkers' paths, still in remarkably good condition, provide easy approaches to the mountains, although these are in contrast to the mountains themselves which are notoriously rough with acres of sharp quartzite and sandstone screes.

Beinn Damh 2959ft/902m

> *Start/Finish:* Loch Torridon Hotel (887542)
> *Maps:* O.S. 1:50,000 Sheets 24 and 25
> *Distance:* 9 miles/14km
> *Time:* 6–7 hours
> *Grading:* An exhilarating mountain walk along a broad ridge.

An Ruadh-stac, a massive quartzite mountain in the Coulin Forest, is seen here from Bealach a'Choire Ghairbh. Photo: Stuart Bramwell.

Beinn Damh rises south of Upper Loch Torridon and just west of the main Coulin Forest peaks; it is an individual and shapely mountain and, missing Munro status by just forty-one feet, it is left mostly undisturbed. Yet, from its northern outlier, Sgurr na Bana Mhoraire, a lofty and stony ridge runs over two miles south to its principal summit. This ridge provides an inspiring mountain walk, worthy of Beinn Damh's inclusion amongst the giants of Torridon.

In its heyday the Ben-Damph estate was thriving deer forest and the adjacent craggy mountains, giving way to well wooded lower slopes, ravines and waterfalls, combined to make a romantic Highland scene. Fortunately the great days of the estate have left a legacy of beautifully constructed stalkers' paths, which make for easy walking into the heart of the mountains.

Beside the road bridge over the Allt Coire Roill, a gate gives access to a path running up through the woods towards Beinn Damh. This path makes a perfect start to the day for it is well drained, gently contoured and carpeted with a soft bed of pine needles. The trees of larch and Caledonian pine are well spaced giving green glades of moss-covered boulders and tangled rhododendrons, while the branches are festooned with lichen. Gaps in the trees allow views down to some magnificent cascades and falls, as the burn thunders through a ravine.

Once clear of the trees the path zig-zags up to the saddle under the north-west ridge of Beinn Damh. It is well worth deviating north along the bouldery ridge to gain the turret-like summit of Sgurr na Bana Mhoraire, which commands a panoramic view of the Sound of Raasay, the Cuillin, the corries of Applecross, Beinn Alligin and Liathach.

Having regained the saddle, proceed south along the whaleback ridge which becomes rough underfoot as the rounded sandstone gives way to angular blocks of quartzite. Height may be saved by following a cairned path which contours two subsidiary summits on the west side.

Beinn Damh's cairn is perched above awesome cliffs. A craggy spur running out to the north-east can be descended by the bold, while, on the southern slopes, light-coloured rocks form a strange stirrup-shaped mark which is clearly visible from the Kishorn road and the Applecross hills. The cliff-girt massif of Maol Chean-dearg rises above Glen a'Bhathaich as an immense sugar loaf.

Scramble down the sharp south-east ridge to gain access to the wide corrie below, then climb back to the Drochaid Coire Roill where you will see a tiny lochan. Here you meet a stalkers' path running back to Loch Torridon.

Floods and frosts have made little impression on this superbly constructed path. Built to take the pressure of hooves of ponies heavily laden with the carcasses of deer, the path is shored up, paved, bridged and drained with runnels of natural stone. Most of Scotland's great estates have such paths, skillfully constructed with picks and shovels and using only rough boulders as building materials. It is a pity that limited money permits only modest employment of such skills in the repair of many of our eroded hill paths. The footpath expert, Robert Aitken, reveals that the rate for constructing a stalkers' path in the Coulin Estate in 1869 was one-and-a-half pence per yard.

The stalkers' path gives a close-up view of the line of east-facing cliffs dropping from the summit ridge of Beinn Damh. Towering up in tiers of black rock, and seamed by deep gullies, the cliffs look very fierce in the fading light of a late afternoon.

Note that the path crosses the Allt Coire Roill just upstream of the waterfall. In wet weather this crossing may be dangerous and you should forego the paths on the east side of the river and keep to the west side on your descent from the Drochaid Coire Roill.

Beinn na h-Eaglaise, 2418ft/737m

Start/Finish: Loch Torridon Hotel (889540)
Maps: O.S. 1:50,000 Sheets 24 and 25
Distance: 7 miles/11km
Time: 4–5 hours
Grading: A rough but easy mountain walk.

In some ways the broad ridge of Beinn na h-Eaglaise mirrors that of its neighbour Beinn Damh south across Coire Roill. It, too, is a chunky sandstone mountain which makes a magnificent belvedere for viewing Liathach and the peaks of the Coulin Forest, yet its ascent is far shorter and less arduous than Beinn Damh.

Beinn na h-Eaglaise has immense bulk and presence and it earns its place amongst the other great peaks of this area of Wester Ross. Nevertheless, if conditions or circumstances do not allow for an ascent of the mountain, excellent stalkers' paths can be followed right round the mountain making a most worthwhile expedition.

Start from the road bridge over the Allt Coire Roill and take the beautiful pine needle-carpeted path through the trees to the open hillside above the gorge. This start is identical to that for the Beinn Damh traverse.

Cross the river by boulder-hopping and continue along the very fine path up the corrie until it levels out. At this point strike straight up the rather boggy, bouldery slopes of Beinn na h-Eaglaise to reach the summit ridge.

The ridge is wide and boulder-strewn and as you walk south to the principal summit you can enjoy the view of the long north-facing crags on Beinn Damh, as well as north across Loch Torridon to Beinn Alligin and Liathach.

From the summit cairn you look straight across the glen to the huge rounded massifs of Maol Chean-dearg and An Ruadh-stac, while the sharply pointed mountains of Sgorr Ruadh and Beinn Liath Mhor look particularly graceful.

Descend south to a group of shallow lochans on the shoulder and then continue down grassy slopes to meet an excellent path near Lochan Domhain (cliffs on the north and east sides preclude a direct descent to the path). Follow the path north until it reaches Loch Torridon at Annat.

Circuit of Beinn na h-Eaglaise

Distance: 8 miles/13km
Time: 4–5 hours

For this very pleasant circuit, which takes you into the heart of a wild, mountainous area, take the Coire Roill path from the road bridge all the way to the top of the pass, the Drochaid Coire Roill.

Head west over a rather boggy and stony area of mountainside, for about half-a-mile to near Loch an Eion, where you meet the excellent path running north to Annat. This path is skilfully constructed and very well maintained by the estate.

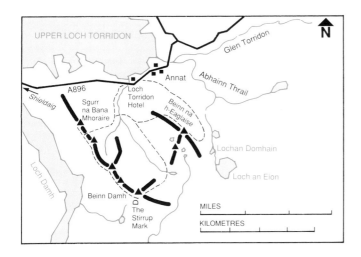

Maol Chean-dearg 3061ft/933m, An Ruadh-stac 2926ft/892m, Meall nan Ceapairean 2132ft/655m

Start/Finish: Coulags (957451)
Map: O.S. 1:50,000 Sheet 25
Distance: 12 miles/19km
Time: 7–8 hours
Grading: A varied walk over rough rocky mountains. Some scrambling involved on An Ruadh-stac.

This not too demanding round makes an excellent introduction to the rather special character of the Coulin Forest/Ben-Damph Forest area. The abrupt and individual peaks are easily approached by stalkers' paths from either Glen Carron or Glen Torridon. Bare rock abounds on An Ruadh-stac while Maol Chean-dearg gives a birds-eye view over the region enabling you to choose further objectives for the future.

For the itinerary from the Glen Carron side of the mountains, park by the road bridge over the Fionn-abhainn near the cottages at Coulags. Take the path signed 'Public Right of Way To Torridon' which runs in front of a white house, keeping close to the burn, and then climbs steadily up the glen.

A wooden bridge soon takes you across to the west side of the burn where, close by, you can still see massive stepping stones in the river bed. A short way further you pass the charming stone cottage of Coire Fionnaraich Bothy, now an open bothy under the care of the Mountain Bothies Association. With an ash tree outside and clean, well furnished and panelled rooms it is a real gem, a proverbial five-star bothy.

The next feature in this fascinating glen is a pointed finger of rock – Clach nan Con-fionn – where the legendary giant called Fionn is said to have tied his hounds. A little further still the path branches at a cairn and you should take the left-hand branch, consisting of white quartzite stones, which climbs up to Bealach a'Choire Ghairbh, under Maol Chean-dearg. This bealach may also be easily reached from Annat by taking the stalkers' path which contours the eastern slopes of Beinn na h-Eaglaise and proceeds to higher ground via Loch an Eion and

Loch Coire an Ruadh-staic.

To bag Maol Chean-dearg you have an easy, but steep, walk up a zig-zag path which winds up the quartzite shoulder to the summit dome. Descend the same way and turn your attention to An Ruadh-stac, an altogether more impressive mountain.

An Ruadh-stac (The Red Stack) would seem to be misnamed because its enormous summit cone is composed of quartzite, scraped smooth by glacial action lower down and frost shattered into screes higher up, while cliffs fall sheer on the north and east sides. In spite of the predominantly rocky terrain thrift and dwarf juniper courageously flourish in the pockets of soil between the boulders.

The slabs to the south can be climbed easily with hands in pockets, for the friction when dry is so good, but this is certainly not true of the top section of chaotically piled sharp and loose boulders. The carefully constructed cairn on the north side of

the summit gives a wonderful view across upper Strath a'Bhathaich to Beinn Damh.

Again return to Bealach a'Choire Ghairbh where there is a group of lochans and climb easily to Meall nan Ceapairean. This is a sandstone mountain and the long south ridge, with constant views across the glen to Fuar Tholl and Sgorr Ruadh, makes a pleasant return route to the road. The ridge carries a luxuriant growth of young heather and, within the space of one minute, we saw a herd of deer, a herd of wild goats and a family of ptarmigan.

Below the ridge the stream courses down in a series of cascades and then enters a wooded ravine. The best descent route follows the north bank and makes for the wooden bridge over the Fionn-abhainn, just over a mile from the road.

The Coire Lair Horseshoe: Fuar Tholl 2975ft/907m, Sgorr Ruadh 3156ft/962m, Beinn Liath Mhor 3034ft/925m

Start/Finish: Achnashellach (004484)
Map: O.S. 1:50,000 Sheet 25
Distance: 12 miles/19km
Time: 9–10 hours
Grading: A long expedition over exceptionally rough mountains involving much ascent and descent but the rewards are commensurate.

This mountain circuit is a classic of its kind. The horseshoe of Coire Lair takes in three highly attractive peaks with a variety of superb features, from stupendous buttresses of clean sandstone, hidden corries, scree gullies and lonesome lochans to a long, high and narrow ridge of white quartzite. The entire area teems with steep rock. Although the circuit is long and arduous the third mountain, Beinn Liath Mhor, can be omitted and an easy escape route taken down Coire Lair back to the road.

Start from the tiny station at Achnashellach and follow the

MILES
KILOMETRES

Loch an Eion
Maol Chean-dearg
Loch Coire an Ruadh-staic
Bealach a' Choire Ghairbh
Loch Coire Fionnaraich
Meall nan Ceapairean
An Ruadh-stac
Clach nan Con-fionn
Bothy
Cnoc nan Each
Fionn abhainn
Achnasheen
A890
Cnoc na h-Atha
Coulags
Lochcarron

Sgurr Dubh, a rock peak on the south side of Glen Torridon, looks majestic from Loch Clair on a sharp spring morning. Photo: Ian Evans.

narrow muddy path which starts on the west side of Station Cottage. The path keeps to the edge of the river Lair and it is overhung with rhododendrons and trees for the first mile before it breaks out onto the hillside, becomes stony, and runs through a stand of remnant Scots pines in a most beautiful and romantic setting.

Where the river thunders through a bottomless gorge the path heads away to the east and climbs quite steeply up into the wide corrie. A cairn marks the place where you must branch left, boulder hop across the river (the crossing may be impossible in very wet weather), and wind your way up towards Bealach Mhoir between Fuar Tholl and Sgorr Ruadh.

Near the top of the pass you will marvel at Mainreachan Coire which falls from the summit of Fuar Tholl and is bounded on the west side by a stupendous buttress of clean sandstone. Leave the path and walk to the tiny lochan under the great buttress; this gives access to two scree slopes, one above the other, which lead safely but tediously to the Fuar Tholl ridge just west of the summit. Cross the plateau to the stone-built trig pillar surrounded by a wind shelter and enjoy the expansive view from one of Scotland's best Corbetts.

Retrace your steps to the top of the scree run and continue over two subsidiary summits of Fuar Tholl before descending nasty, steep, loose boulders and scree to Bealach Mhoir where there are some confusing hummocks and a marker cairn beside the path.

An easy climb takes you on to the sharp summit of Sgorr Ruadh where you meet a narrow quartzite ridge which soon gives way to brilliant white screes.

When the screes peter out leave the path and descend grassy slopes to a lochan at the head of Coire Lair. This is the crossing point for the path linking Achnashellach with Annat which provides an escape route for the weary.

The quartzite ridge of Beinn Liath Mhor towers above the lochan and sandstone cliffs seemingly block the ascent. But these cliffs can be by-passed on the right (east) and steep slopes climbed to a tiny lochan nestling in a hollow. A very narrow cairned path winds a tortuous route through another band of

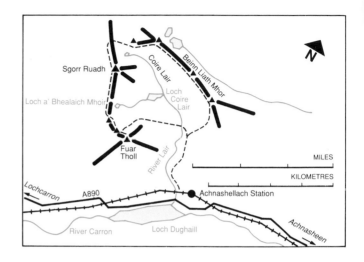

cliffs to the quartzite upper shoulder of Beinn Liath Mhor.

A pile of boulders marks the true summit of Beinn Liath Mhor and the ridge running east is extremely tiresome with excruciatingly sharp, confused rocks requiring close concentration. This is a pity because there are superb views south into the inner corries of Sgorr Ruadh and Fuar Tholl.

The ridge is well over a mile long and rises to a subsidiary sandstone summit before it dips to a low bealach and then changes to bright white quartzite for the final haul to Point 876m, the eastern top. A shattered rock castle sprouts from this final section but it is easily turned.

The descent from Point 876m is tricky because the direct route is blocked by crags. It is best to keep slightly north of east on heather and boulders until the angle eases. A tiny stone stalkers' shelter, like an igloo, marks the start of a narrow path which eventually takes you down to the main track coming up from Coulin, just a short distance from its junction with the morning's approach track from Achnashellach.

Sgurr Dubh 2566ft/782m and Sgorr nan Lochan Uaine 2864ft/873m

Start: Loch Clair (003581)
Finish: Coire Dubh Mor car park (958568)
Map: O.S. 1:50,000 Sheet 25
Distance: 10 miles/16km
Time: 6 hours
Grading: An enjoyable and remote mountain walk involving some very rough ground.

These two hills, occupying the no-man's-land between the giants of Torridon and the Coulin Forest, tend to be neglected by the walker. However, Sgorr nan Lochan Uaine in particular is a most intriguing mountain with lots of delightful features and, in the almost guaranteed absence of other humans, it can make a thoroughly rewarding expedition.

Sgurr Dubh is a shapely, conical hill of broken cliffs and scree slopes and it is quite prominent to the driver proceeding west down Glen Torridon. It can be climbed from almost anywhere. I have even ascended it straight up from the Ling Hut, but here I shall describe an expedition linking Loch Clair with the Ling Hut which combines Sgurr Dubh with Sgorr nan Lochan Uaine.

Take the private road that runs from the A896 to Loch Clair, crosses the river and passes through luxuriant growths of rhododendrons on its way to Coulin Lodge.

Behind the Lodge a group of outbuildings gives access to a narrow path which hugs the side of the Allt na Luib and climbs up through a lovely stand of Scots pines. Very soon you cross to the north side of the burn by a wooden bridge but scattered remnant pines persist for some way up the glen.

The stalkers' path is a real boon as the hillside is deep in tangled heather and boulders, but it eventually stops suddenly at about 500m at a stone-built bivvy (where I once found a box of matches and a Mars bar wrapped in a polythene bag for needy travellers).

Head uphill, in a westward direction, crossing numerous dry stream beds containing white quartzite boulders. Tiny lochans abound in the hollows amongst the hillocks on the plateau between Sgurr Dubh and Sgorr nan Lochan Uaine. Turn north and ascend the boulders to Sgurr Dubh, retrace your steps to the plateau and begin the long climb to Sgorr nan Lochan Uaine, which is a fine conical peak of loose quartzite boulders. The summit itself, which carries a circular windbreak, strangely reverts to grass.

Very steep scrambly slopes of loose quartzite lead down to a lochan on the north shoulder. Then make your way north-west down inexorable quartzite screes, broken cliffs, bluffs and boulders which seem to go on for ever. You cannot relax your concentration for a second on this very rough hillside.

Eventually you arrive at lower ground, in an area of unusually humpy moraines, where you meet the stalkers' path running to the A896 near the Coire Dubh Mor car park. The path passes the whitewashed Ling Hut, a private climbing hut owned by the Scottish Mountaineering Club.

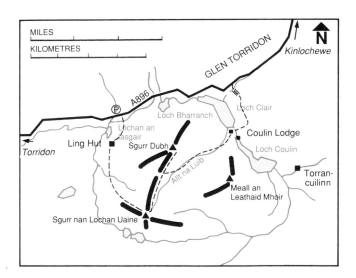

Coulin Pass

Distance: 9 miles/15km
Time: 4–5 hours

This traditional right-of-way crosses the Coulin Forest between Glen Carron and Glen Torridon and gives a magnificently varied walk through beautiful glen and mountain scenery. It is not an arduous walk, for the summit of the pass is only 940ft/286m and the path is excellent throughout.

Transport must be organised at the end of the day, but this task is well worthwhile because the walk thoroughly deserves its reputation as a classic that gives the best possible introduction to this wild area of the North West Highlands.

From Achnashellach station cross the line carefully and take the wide track, signed 'Coulin Pass', which runs eastwards through the forestry plantation.

Soon after emerging from the trees you arrive at the top of the pass and can enjoy the impressive view north to Beinn Eighe. Continue walking over the open moorland until you reach the stone bridge at the junction of the Easan Dorcha and the Allt Doire Bheithe. This is an enchanting spot with waterfalls and Scots pines growing on the sides of the burns.

At Loch Coulin you can take paths on either the north or south banks, but if you choose the south side you should cross the wooden bridge over the reedy north end of the loch to regain the metalled road.

One of Scotland's hidden gems. The triple buttresses of Coire Mhic Fhearchair plunge down from the summit ridge of Beinn Eighe. Photo: Richard Gibbens.

3 TORRIDON

Glen Torridon stretches for eleven miles from Kinlochewe to Loch Torridon and the scenery rivals even Glen Coe for grandeur. The famous Scottish writer, W. H. Murray, reckons that Torridon exhibits more mountain beauty than any other district in Scotland, including Skye.

The two mighty monoliths, Liathach and Beinn Eighe, each boasting a long and sharp ridge, present unrelentingly steep slopes on the west side of the glen. Liathach is terraced with walls of old sandstone which soar upwards in ledges and buttresses, while Beinn Eighe is clothed in white quartzite screes which give the appearance of snow when the sun glances off them.

West of Liathach rises Beinn Alligin whose horseshoe ridge and deep corrie look so impressive when seen across Loch Torridon from the road to Shieldaig. Alligin is characterised by a deep, slanting cleft which splits the face of the principal summit, Sgurr Mhor, and a line of rock teeth called the Horns on the east side of the corrie.

The fourth member of the Torridon quartet, Beinn Dearg, lies behind Liathach and delineates the southern boundary of the Flowerdale Forest. Beinn Dearg too has sections of airy ridge, interspersed with sandstone towers.

It is heartening to know that a large area of Torridon is owned by the National Trust for Scotland. This includes the whole of Beinn Alligin and Liathach and the southern slopes of Beinn Dearg and Beinn Eighe from their summit ridges. In addition an area of 4,800 hectares, which contains most of Beinn Eighe and extends to Loch Maree, is a National Nature Reserve administered by Scottish Natural Heritage.

Torridon needs special designation and status to protect and extend the areas of relic deciduous woodlands, and stands of Caledonian pines, which make them so precious scientifically and scenically and such a delight to explore.

Visitors' centres provide a comprehensive selection of information on the Torridon area. The SNT centre is at the west end of Glen Torridon and the SNH centre on the Loch Maree side of Kinlochewe.

Beinn Alligin 3232ft/985m

Start/Finish: Coire Mhic Nobuil road bridge (867577)
Maps: O.S. 1:50,000 Sheet 24 and O.S. 1:25,000 Outdoor Leisure Map – 'The Cuillin and Torridon Hills'
Distance: 9 miles/14km
Time: 7 hours
Grading: A fine traverse of a lofty mountain ridge involving some mild scrambling. Much more serious under full winter conditions.

Of the giants of Torridon, Liathach and Beinn Eighe engender awe, with their uncompromisingly steep shoulders, deep corries and towering buttresses of striated sandstone and quartzite. Beinn Alligin, which rises above Loch Torridon a few miles west of Liathach, is altogether more modest. It too throws down sandstone cliffs from narrow ridges, but it presents a friendlier face to the world. When Beinn Alligin is seen from across the blue water of Loch Torridon, bathed in spring sunshine and capped with snow, it fully justifies its nickname of the Jewel of Torridon. The mountain is owned by the National Trust for Scotland and access is unrestricted at all times of the year.

From the car park beside the bridge over the Abhainn Coire

Mhic Nobuil, the simplest way is to take the stalkers' path on the west side of the burn which runs besides woods of Scots pine, birch, alder, holly and rhododendron. After about half-a-mile strike off to the left and make your way up a rather boggy path which leads up into Coir' nan Laogh, zig-zagging beside the stream and eventually depositing you on the desolate summit plateau of Tom na Gruagaich.

But a far more interesting ascent is to start up the west bank of the Abhainn Coire Mhic Nobuil and strike straight up the tussocks of coarse grass and heather, winding your way through bluffs of Torridonian sandstone to the nose of Na Fasreidhnean. This thrusting spur makes up the west edge of Coir' nan Laogh; it looks fearsomely steep but when tackled directly gives easy scrambling, in some exposed places, and you hardly know you are gaining height until suddenly you reach the south ridge of Tom na Gruagaich. Throughout the ascent you can enjoy expansive views to the south and west; views which are restricted on the alternative, Coir' nan Laogh, route.

A stone built O.S. pillar marks the summit of Tom na Gruagaich which has a line of crags overlooking the fearsome corrie of Toll a'Mhadaidh, falling sheer from Alligin's main summit. Descend quite steeply for 500ft beside towering precipices of ledgy sandstone to reach a saddle.

Keep to the corrie rim as you ascend Sgurr Mhor and marvel at the incredible cleft which splits the face of Alligin, a sizeable slice of rock having fallen away in a previous era. A wide fan of scree and a chaos of boulders on the corrie floor is evidence of this remarkable rock fall.

From the summit of Sgurr Mhor a magnificent vista opens out: west across the Sound of Raasay to Quirang, south to Beinn Damh and Applecross, north to the remote Flowerdale Forest and east to the nearby rock pinnacles known as the Horns of Alligin.

Descend steepish boulder slopes on the east of Sgurr Mhor to a bealach at 757m. From here an easy way down southwards into the corrie can be effected if required, but the three Rathains or Horns which come next can be the highlight of the day and should not be missed.

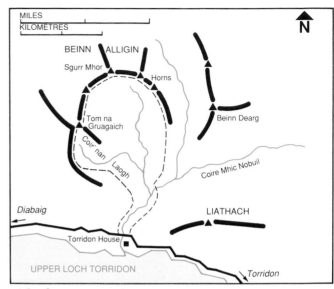

The first Horn can be climbed directly. The sandstone crest gives an exposed scramble but various traverse paths on the south side enable the faint hearted to avoid the difficulties. From the final Horn a cairned path runs down to Loch a'Bhealaich; it is best to stick with this path for it follows the line of least resistance through a belt of broken crags.

The Allt a'Bhealaich is crossed by a wooden bridge and the path on the east side of the burn leads down into Coire Mhic Nobuil. The burn tumbles down in a succession of beautiful falls and cascades with numerous enticing pools for a swim on a hot day.

Another wooden bridge carries you over the Abhainn Coire Mhic Nobuil to the path on the east side which meanders through the woods above a deep gorge back to the car park.

A view north-east from Beinn Alligin over the 'Horns' to Beinn Dearg and Beinn Eighe. Photo: Alan O'Brien.

Beinn Dearg 2999ft/914m

Start: Coire Dubh Mor car park (958568)
Finish: Coire Mhic Nobuil road bridge (867577)
Maps: O.S. 1:50,000 Sheet 25 and O.S. 1:25,000 Outdoor Leisure Map –
'The Cuillin and Torridon Hills'
Distance: 11 miles/18km
Time: 7–8 hours
Grading: A fine mountain traverse set amidst superb scenery. Experience
and some scrambling ability essential.

Beinn Dearg is tucked away behind Liathach on the southern edge of the Flowerdale Forest. Although it is only possible to catch glimpses of the peak from the Torridon road it is no Cinderella mountain; it misses Munro status by just a whisker and its long and narrow summit ridge, overlooking deep corries and sandstone cliffs, guarantees its rightful inclusion in the mighty Torridon quartet along with Beinn Alligin, Beinn Eighe and Liathach.

Beinn Dearg can be climbed in a long day from Am Feur Loch, walking in via Loch na h-Oidhche as described in the chapter on Beinn an Eoin and Baosbheinn, but a much shorter expedition is to include Beinn Dearg's ascent in a walk through Coire Mhic Nobuil from Glen Torridon to Torridon House.

From the Coire Dubh Mor car park walk under the eastern end of Liathach to the cairn marking the path which turns off to Coire Mhic Fhearchair. Now keep to the north side of the group of lochans at the watershed under Beinn Dearg's eastern summit, Carn na Feola.

Although on the north and east sides of Carn na Feola crags block the ascent, a fairly simple but steep scramble on the south side, above Loch Grobaig, leads directly to the summit.

Head west to Beinn Dearg's main summit along one of Scotland's most enjoyable high ridges. The views to Flowerdale and south to the northern corries of Liathach are unsurpassed. Just before reaching the top, the ridge narrows and some quite tricky castles of rock must be climbed or by-passed. The large cairn on Beinn Dearg's summit has been built to ensure that some part of the mountain attains the magic height of 3000ft.

The sharp ridge now dips to the north and then rises to the flat-topped Stuc Loch na Cabhaig which looks across the Bealach a'Chomhla to the Horns of Alligin. Descend north-west to avoid the worst of the crags, picking your way carefully to lower ground. Continue southwards over the rough, stony hillside to meet a path leading to Coire Mhic Nobuil, barely a mile from the car park near Torridon House.

Liathach 3458ft/1054m

Start: Coire Dubh Mor car park (958568)
Finish: Torridon village (898563)
Maps: O.S. 1:50,000 Sheet 25 and O.S. 1:25,000 Outdoor Leisure Map –
'The Cuillin and Torridon Hills'
Distance: 9 Miles/15km
Time: 7 hours
Grading: A magnificent high mountain traverse which can become serious
in bad conditions. Not recommended for inexperienced walkers.

Liathach towers above Glen Torridon as a stupendous monolith of bare rock, and when it is clothed in fresh snow and viewed across Loch Clair (one of the classic mountain views in Britain) it looks impregnable.

I am reminded of Ruskin's lines:

'These great cathedrals of the earth,
with their gates of rock, pavements
of cloud, choirs of stream and stone,
altars of snow, and vaults of purple
traversed by the continual stars.'

In winter the traverse of Liathach is a major mountaineering venture, but in good conditions it can be safely accomplished by experienced hill walkers with a good head for heights and some scrambling ability. However, once embarked upon the traverse of the three mile summit ridge you are committed to finish it or return by the route of ascent, for the ridge is poised over rock buttresses and towers and few escape routes can be found.

*Climbers approach Spidean a'Choire Leith on a winter traverse of Liathach.
Photo: Richard Gibbens.*

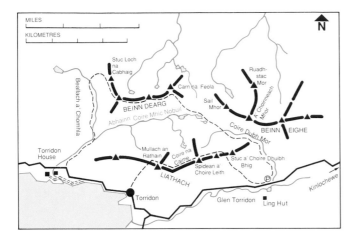

Start from the Coire Dubh Mor car park in Glen Torridon. Since the eastern top of Liathach, Stuc a'Choire Dhuibh Bhig, is crag-bound on the Coire Dubh side, it is best to ascend Coire Liath Mhor on the south side to gain access to the ridge proper.

Walk down the road for a mile and then strike up the steep hillside beside the Allt an Doire Ghairbh. For a few hundred feet there is a rough path, but then a professionally improved section leads you up into the upper corrie through rock outcrops until you arrive at the bealach under Bidean Toll a'Mhuic. Purists can make a short excursion to Liathach's eastern top, Stuc a'Choire Dhuibh Bhig.

An easy but narrow ridge runs over the tops of Bidean Toll a'Mhuic to the base of the impressive triangular-shaped face of Spidean a'Choire Leith. The ascent of this, the main summit of Liathach at 3458ft/1054m, is rough and bouldery but quite straightforward.

Sgurr Ban and Sgurr nan Fhir Duibhe, the two eastern summits of Beinn Eighe, reflected in Loch Clair. Photo: Ian Evans.

As you descend westwards from Spidean a'Choire Leith you look across the depths of Coire na Caime to the splintered pinnacles running north from Mullach an Rathain, Liathach's second separate Munro at 3356ft/1023m. A winter ascent of this pinnacle ridge is incomparably described by W. H. Murray in his book *Undiscovered Scotland*.

But before you can begin the climb to Mullach an Rathain you must negotiate the notorious Pinnacles of Am Fasarinen. Here the ridge narrows to a razor edge; the drop on the north side is sheer and the exposure is awesome, yet the difficulties are short lived and can be avoided altogether by using a detour path one hundred feet below.

After the Pinnacles the ridge broadens out and becomes grassy for a stretch before rising again to the boulder strewn summit of Mullach an Rathain. Pause to enjoy the magnificent rock scenery and the close-up views of Beinn Alligin, Beinn Dearg and Beinn Damh.

Descend the quartzite ridge westwards for half-a-mile and then, on the south side, you will find a scree shoot which can be run right down to the heather just above Torridon village. If you have not been able to organise transport at Torridon it is three miles back through Glen Torridon to the Coire Dubh Mor car park.

Beinn Eighe 3314ft/1010m

> *Start: Coire Dubh Mor car park (958568)*
> *Finish: Kinlochewe (028620)*
> *Maps: O.S. 1:50,000 Sheet 25 and O.S. 1:25,000 Outdoor Leisure Map - 'The Cuillin and Torridon Hills'*
> *Distance: 13 miles/21km*
> *Time: 8–9 hours*
> *Grading: A long traverse over one of Scotland's grandest mountains. Some rock scrambling is involved and a safety rope should be carried.*

Beinn Eighe rises above Glen Torridon in ever steepening slopes of grey quartzite and it has a commanding presence even if it appears slightly dull. But when seen from the Flowerdale Forest

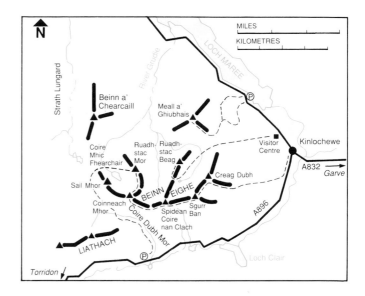

or from any vantage point on the west side its true character can be appreciated: rocky spurs thrust out from the sharp main ridge, enclosing deep corries with precipitous headwalls. The most westerly of these is the stupendous Coire Mhic Fhearchair which has a reputation for dramatic rock scenery second to none in Scotland.

The complete traverse of Beinn Eighe's main ridge is one of the classic mountain expeditions in Britain; it is longer than Liathach's ridge and equally serious and committing, with few easy escape routes. Several sections of the ridge could require the use of a safety rope in winter conditions.

Note that the area of Beinn Eighe east of the summit ridge is a National Nature Reserve, but access is permitted except on

Next page: Fresh overnight snow blankets the Beinn Eighe massif, seen in this December picture from near Coulin Lodge. Photo: Jim Teesdale.

certain days in the deer stalking season. Details are available from the Nature Reserve Information Centre near Kinlochewe.

Start the walk from the car park at the mouth of Coire Dubh Mor which divides the massifs of Liathach and Beinn Eighe. A path, which passes a ruined cottage near the road, leads up the glen keeping to the west side of the burn. It climbs to 1200ft, before passing under the steep eastern abutment of Liathach where it flattens out and crosses the burn. The path then divides and you should take the right-hand branch, which is cairned and makes a rising traverse across the very rough shoulder of Sail Mhor. The left-hand branch descends Coire Mhic Nobuil on the north side of Liathach.

As you work round to the north side of Sail Mhor you pass under towering buttresses of red sandstone and then, quite suddenly, you are in Coire Mhic Fhearchair confronted by one of the most dramatic sights in all Scotland. A dark lochan spills over the lip of the corrie in a cascade of waterfalls, while above the lochan rise three giant buttresses of white quartzite standing on a plinth of sandstone. The 1300ft cliffs provide excellent rock climbing on clean and sound quartzite. The left-hand (easternmost) buttress gives the easiest climb at about 'Difficult' standard.

The view looking west out of the corrie is equally delightful, but in complete contrast to the triple buttresses. The hills of the Flowerdale Forest rise abruptly from the flat, boggy floor, Beinn a'Chearcaill and Beinn an Eoin being particularly prominent.

Beinn Eighe's highest summit, Ruadh-stac Mor, lies on the east side of Coire Mhic Fhearchair and it is an easy but exasperating 1500ft climb up the scree slopes to the summit cairn. The ridge is now followed south to Coinneach Mhor which is a better viewpoint than Ruadh-stac Mor. Liathach's sharp summits and pinnacles stand out across Glen Dubh Mor, and further west Beinn Alligin, with its characteristic cleft, and Beinn Dearg complete the quartet of giants. To the south Mam Sodhail and Carn Eige can be seen rising above the Glen Strathfarrar ridge.

If you intend to climb all the tops of Beinn Eighe, a steep and scrambly descent should be made west from Coinneach Mhor to the south ridge of Sail Mhor, whence an easy climb leads to its summit.

The main ridge east of Coinneach Mhor meanders easily to Spidean Coire nan Clach where subsidiary spurs run off to the north and south. After another dip the ridge rises to Sgurr Ban and then to Sgurr nan Fhir Duibhe where excitement commences.

To reach Creag Dhubh, the final and most easterly summit on the Beinn Eighe ridge, a spiky rock ridge, marked Bodaich Dubh Beinn Eighe on the map, must be traversed. These pinnacles are known as the Black Men, their negotiation requires care and there is no easy way round. However, *in extremis*, a path can be found contouring under the rocks on the south side.

At Creag Dhubh the ridge divides and you should take the right-hand, eastern branch. For 1500ft the descent is extremely tiresome as you pick your way down the boulder fields, but when you reach the Allt a'Chuirn the hillside becomes firm and peaty. A path on the north side of the burn leads to the road less than a mile south of Kinlochewe.

Other Worthwhile Routes

The above traverse can be shortened considerably, and the difficult scrambling section over the Black Men of Sgurr nan Fhir Duibhe avoided altogether, by a change of route.

From the trig pillar on the summit of Spidean Coire nan Clach descend southwards over the subsidiary Stuc Coire an Laoigh. You can then continue the descent either south-west down Coire nan Clach to Glen Dubh Mor, or south-east down Coire an Laoigh to meet the marked path leading to the Torridon road near Loch Bharranch.

Previous page: Wreaths of cloud drift from the summit ridge of Liathach, seen here across Glen Torridon from Sgurr Dubh. Photo: Alan O'Brien.

Ruadh-stac Beag 2940ft/896m

Start/Finish: Beinn Eighe NNR Visitors' Centre (020630)
Maps: O.S. 1:50,000 Sheet 19 and O.S. 1:25,000 Outdoor Leisure Map –
'The Cuillin and Torridon Hills'
Distance: 10 miles/16km
Time: 5–6 hours
Grading: A surprisingly barren, steep and inhospitable outlier of Beinn
Eighe.

This monolithic mountain is a northerly off-shoot of Beinn Eighe but its ascent is rarely included in the main ridge traverse which is already a long and arduous expedition.

However, Ruadh-stac Beag makes a thoroughly worthwhile objective from Kinlochewe, for not only is the approach through the National Nature Reserve which provides a host of interesting features but it gives an insight into the very wild and lonely northern corries of Beinn Eighe. In addition, the mountain is something of a fortress with stout defences and its south-west ridge provides the only foolproof means of ascent, and even this ridge is of steep, sharp boulders. In fact the general appearance of Ruadh-stac Beag from the south and east is of relentless slopes of quartzite screes topped with a line of crags; its name 'Small Red Hill' seems to be a misnomer.

An excellent stalkers' path leaves the A832 near the Beinn Eighe Nature Reserve Visitor's Centre, passes through a belt of trees, crosses a stream by a wooden bridge and then breaks out onto the open hillside.

The path is composed of loose quartzite stones and it snakes easily up towards Creag Dhubh, the eastern extremity of Beinn Eighe. After passing through a gate in the deer fence and crossing the Eas a'Bhadain Duinn it swings away towards Meall a'Ghiubhais. From this point you can head straight towards Ruadh-stac Beag across a remarkably bare and open quartzite boulder field which can have changed little since the glaciers retreated 10,000 years ago.

It is rough and hard walking with only a few patches of heather and dwarf juniper, but the going becomes a little easier beside the stream which runs under the east face of Ruadh-stac Beag. On my ascent we climbed the inexorably steep scree slopes, wove our way through the crags at the top and reached the stony summit plateau very near the tiny cairn. But the route was marginal and it would have been better to have continued southwards, beside the stream, to the base of the easier south ridge.

Enjoy excellent views into the Toll Ban and Ruadh-staca corries of Beinn Eighe, as well as across the Flowerdale Forest to Baosbheinn, and then scramble down the south ridge. A slight variation on the return route is to follow the stream down to meet the path of ascent under the north-east ridge of Ruadh-stac Beag.

The Beinn Eighe Mountain Trail and Meall a'Ghiubhais 2881ft/878m

Start/Finish: Loch Mareeside (001650)
Maps: O.S. 1:50,000 Sheet 19 and O.S. 1:25,000 Outdoor Leisure Map –
'The Cuillin and Torridon Hills'
Distance: 6 miles/10km
Time: 4–5 hours
Grading: A simple walk, mostly along a well marked path.

Scottish Natural Heritage have built a mountain trail from Loch Mareeside, up through the incomparable pine woods of Coille na Glas Leitire (part of the Beinn Eighe National Nature Reserve) to a Conservation Cairn at a height of 550m which is a notable viewpoint. An easy extension of this walk is the ascent of Meall a'Ghiubhais, an even better viewpoint and a more challenging objective than the Conservation Cairn.

The trail begins from the car park beside Loch Maree two-and-a-half miles north of Kinlochewe. A very informative booklet is available which describes the important features on the trail.

Glas Leitire is one of the most important relic pine woods in Scotland, several of the older trees being over 350 years old. Their beauty enhances any scene and they provide the perfect foreground for stunning views across Loch Maree to Slioch. The trail zig-zags through the trees crossing the Alltan Mhic Eoghainn near a fine waterfall.

Since the trail has been built by various conservation bodies to be suitable for all-comers, it has been cleared of loose rocks and boulders which have been piled in numerous cairns beside the path. It is a good example of the destruction of wild places by the human race in the furtherance of access, although in this case the aim is honourable, to allow the interested public to see an important NNR, which is financed by government funds.

Above the tree-line the landscape is open with areas of shattered grey quartzite, juniper, mountain azalea, crowberry, alpine bearberry and various club mosses and mountain sedges. It is a prime example of 'dwarf shrub heath' vegetation typical of arctic tundra.

The large Conservation Cairn is something of an eyesore and hardly lives up to its name, but it is said to command a view of thirty-one 3000ft mountains.

It is now less than an hour's walk to the twin summits of Meall a'Ghiubhais, skirting the tiny lochans on the east side and climbing easily up the steep grass and boulder fields. The south summit, which carries a substantial cairn, is the highest and it provides excellent views of the great northern corries of Beinn Eighe, although one is denied a view into Coire Mhic Fhearchair. The vast boiler plate slabs on the north face of Ruadh-stac Beag are very impressive. A'Mhaighdean and the distant ridge of An Teallach can be glimpsed through the gap between Slioch and Beinn Lair.

From the Conservation Cairn the trail descends beside the Allt na h'Airighe gorge, a deep and dripping chasm which is heavily vegetated because of shelter from the elements and protection from grazing.

The last stretch of the trail ambles pleasantly through mixed woodlands and rock outcrops back to the car park.

Baosbheinn (left) and Beinn an Eoin (right) dominate the lonely Flowerdale Forest. Photo: Iain Brown.

4 FLOWERDALE FOREST

Flowerdale Forest: the name alone should be sufficiently emotive to entice walkers to this remote region of Wester Ross. Yet few visitors venture west of the Torridon giants. Having traversed Beinn Eighe, Liathach and Beinn Alligin they return home sated with superlatives, or make for sandy coves at Gairloch and Gruinard to relax.

When viewed from Torridon's lofty heights much of the Flowerdale Forest appears flat and boggy, a desolate area crisscrossed by rivulets and patterned with a mosaic of tiny lochans, a bleak and watery world, not unlike Coigach to the north. But the quality of the landscape is transformed by three superb individual peaks which rear up from the sandstone bedrock. Baosbheinn, Beinn an Eoin and Beinn a'Chearcaill have fine ridges linking their principal summits which throw down steep, gully seamed shoulders enclosing wild corries and dark lochans.

I shall never forget the view of Flowerdale from Coire Mhic Fhearchair one sparkling March day when the peaks were plastered in snow, the sun glinted on the ice-covered lochans and Loch na h-Oidhche reflected the arctic blue of the sky. The scene was so beautiful that it made a greater impression on me than Coire Mhic Fhearchair's famous triple buttresses themselves.

The Flowerdale peaks are not easily won. A stalkers' path runs in for six miles from the Gairloch-Loch Maree road to a boathouse at the northern end of Loch na h-Oidhche, but from there onwards the going is trackless. You must pick your own route up the steep, rough slopes of heather and boulders and negotiate your own way through the crags and along the ridges.

Beinn an Eoin 2805ft/855m and Baosbheinn 2871ft/875m

> *Start/Finish:* Am Feur Loch on the A832 (856720)
> *Maps:* O.S. 1:50,000 Sheet 19 and O.S. 1:25,000 Outdoor Leisure Map – 'The Cuillin and Torridon Hills'
> *Distance:* 15 miles/24km
> *Time:* 8 hours
> *Grading:* A long expedition into remote mountainous country. Two high and exposed ridges must be traversed which could be problematical in severe weather conditions.

A stalkers' path starts from Am Feur Loch and winds its way into the heart of Flowerdale. For much of the way it follows the Abhainn a'Gharbh Choire, a lively, foaming torrent which rushes down from Loch na h-Oidhche in a series of falls and cascades.

After two hours walking you arrive at the robust, corrugated iron-roofed boathouse beside Loch na h-Oidhche which can provide some temporary shelter in bad weather. A steep scramble takes you to the northern end of the Beinn an Eoin ridge, the last hundred feet through a fringe of weathered sandstone outcrops.

In stormy weather the scene below can be dramatic with water spouts racing across the surface of Loch na h-Oidhche to spend their energy on the flanks of Baosbheinn.

Shafts of light play on the islets and bays of Loch Maree, deer graze Coire na Ciche, the stupendous massif of Slioch towers up in the east while, away to the far north, the jagged silhouette of An Teallach is outlined against the horizon.

The summit of Beinn an Eoin is at the south end of the ridge where it narrows to give a touch of exposure. Broken slopes on the west side can be easily descended to the estate-owned cottage of Poca-Buidhe. This low stone bothy nestles amongst huge boulders, merging almost invisibly into the background.

The south ridge of Baosbheinn lies a mile to the west across a barren wilderness, liberally sprinkled with boulders and shallow pools, but the going is surprisingly easy over large areas of glacier scoured sandstone slabs.

Grassy slopes lead up to sandstone formations on Ceann Beag, the southern summit. Thereafter the ridge continues in a series of rocky turrets to the main top, Sgorr Dubh. Wonderful close-up views are enjoyed of Beinn Alligin and the Horns across Loch a'Bhealaich.

The splendid airy ridge of Baosbheinn runs on northwards over several minor tops to Creag an Fhithich where it ends abruptly in cliffs. Descend the eastern slopes to the Abhainn a'Gharbh Choire where you regain the approach path.

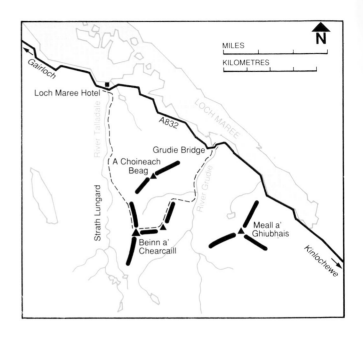

Beinn a'Chearcaill and the Talladale Gorge, 2397ft/725m

Start: Bridge of Grudie (963678)
Finish: Loch Maree Hotel (913704)
Maps: O.S. 1:50,000 Sheet 19 and O.S. 1:25,000 Ourtdoor Leisure Map – 'The Cuillin and Torridon Hills'
Distance: 10 miles/16km
Time: 5 hours
Grading: An easy ascent of an unfashionable mountain, but one that is a superb viewpoint. A rough and trackless return alongside a magnificent gorge.

This very fine and reasonably accessible mountain does not even attain Corbett status; but this is to its advantage because it suffers no paths or muddy boot prints and it gives you a wonderful sense of space and isolation. To return alongside the Talladale Gorge and some exceptional falls is to experience one of the wildest natural features in the North West Highlands.

The stalkers' path from Bridge of Grudie leads you high above the rushing Grudie river which runs between birch trees and Caledonian pines. As you gain height enticing views unfold of the northern corries of Beinn Eighe and it is tempting to stay on the path to the top of the glen. But Beinn a'Chearcaill is a sandstone mountain and quite rocky, and to avoid the crags you should follow the burn up Coire Briste to a high plateau north of the main summit.

The plateau is extensive and is littered with sandstone boulders while lochans fill every pocket and hollow; good grazing makes it popular with deer. The actual summit of Beinn a'Chearcaill is a smooth tabletop of red sandstone carrying a small and untidy cairn. As can be imagined from its position, it is a superb viewpoint for Beinn Eighe (looking right into Coire Mhic Fhearchair), Liathach, Beinn Dearg, Beinn Alligin and Beinn an Eoin. Across Loch Maree the cliffs on A'Mhaighdean are prominent beyond Beinn Lair.

Descend the broad north ridge for nearly a mile and then plough down westwards, through the heather and moorgrass, to the bank of the Talladale river in Srath Lungard. At this point the river is wide, very deep and slow moving and it is quite unfordable unless you are prepared to swim.

There is no vestige of a path along the river bank and you must push through deep coarse grass for two miles until the landscape changes dramatically.

Without warning the river drops into a huge amphitheatre ringed by cliffs. The falls are about seventy feet high and the water plunges into a deep, dark pool. With Caledonian pines, birches, rowan trees and heather growing on the sides of the cliffs the scene is exceptionally beautiful and romantic and is probably not surpassed by anything in this guidebook. It is the climax to the day, yet gets no mention in any other book I have read.

The Talladale river continues its headlong rush into Loch Maree down a deep and well wooded gorge which is two miles in length. There is no alternative but to traverse the trackless hillside keeping well back from the gorge; it is tough going through deep heather, grass and bog myrtle.

As you approach Loch Maree you can descend to the riverside and complete the walk through shady woods of oak and alder. The Loch Maree hotel is near at hand for refreshments but, if no transport awaits you, there is a three mile walk back along the road to your starting place at Bridge of Grudie.

N.B. In the 1980s, run-of-river hydro-electric schemes were proposed for both the Grudie and Talladale rivers. Shocked and angry, the conservation bodies in Britain united in vehement opposition to the plans and, thankfully, they were soon dropped.

Tollie Farm to Slattadale Walk

Distance: 6 miles/10km
Time: 3 hours

Although the road from Poolewe to Kinlochewe makes a long diversion through Gairloch and alongside the river Kerry, a delightful short cut can be made by walkers using an excellent six mile long path linking Tollie Farm with Slattadale. The walk takes about three hours and transport should be arranged for return from Slattadale because the local bus service is infrequent.

Park near the signpost on the A832 and follow the path over rough moorland on the west side of Creag Mhor Thollaidh. You pass several waterfalls and cascades and a number of burns must be boulder hopped. From the watershed Loch Maree appears in all its majesty with tree-covered islands and distant Slioch dominating the scene. This is one of the great views in Scotland.

A descent to Slattadale follows where a gate provides entrance to the forest. A clearing in the trees gives an even better view of the islands but sadly not to Isle Maree, the most romantic of them all, which lies close to the Letterewe shore.

Isle Maree is well wooded and used to be the scene of pagan rites. There are also the remains of a seventh-century chapel, some ancient headstones, a well whose water is said to cure madness and a wishing tree visited by Queen Victoria in 1877.

A car park and picnic area beside the loch and just below the main road marks the end of the walk.

5 THE GREAT WILDERNESS

The huge tract of mountainous country which extends eighteen miles north–south from Little Loch Broom to Loch Maree and twenty miles east–west from the Fannichs to Poolewe is popularly known as the Great Wilderness. It includes the vast deer forests of Kinlochewe, Letterewe, Fisherfield, Dundonnell and Strathnasheallag.

Fortunately the area has not yet suffered from the ravages of afforestation, and there is a bare minimum of scarring from bulldozed tracks, for generations of sportsmen have approached the hills by boat, using Loch Maree, Loch a'Bhraoin, the Fionn Loch and Loch na Sealga for their access. Apart from a few cottages on the periphery there is no permanent habitation within the the boundaries of the Great Wilderness.

The landscape is predominantly rocky and, with glaciers having gouged out deep corries and hollows, there is an abundance of lonely lochs. A complex mixture of rocks from a long series of geological eras has led to a wide variety of mountain features: sharply serrated ridges, soaring cliffs of gneiss, sandstone terraces, plateaus of shattered quartzite and grassy glens.

Thus the Great Wilderness is a Mecca for the hill walker and mountaineer, a priceless reserve for wild life and flora and a fascinating relic of the old Highlands which has changed little since the retreat of the ice sheet nearly 10,000 years ago.

Slioch 3215ft/980m

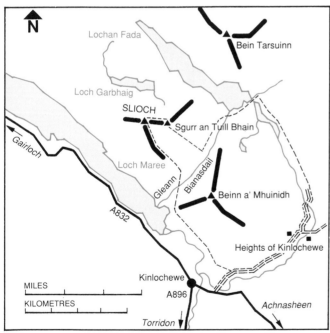

Walkers pause to admire the cornice on Sail Liath while approaching An Teallach from Corrie Hallie. Photo: Richard Gilbert.

> *Start/Finish:* Kinlochewe (028619)
> *Map:* O.S. 1:50,000 Sheet 19
> *Distance:* 18 miles/29km
> *Time:* 8–9 hours
> *Grading:* A classic mountain walk. Most of the route follows a path, but some rough terrain must be negotiated on Slioch itself.

If there is one view which sums up the beauty of the West Highland scene, it is that of snow-capped Slioch seen across the blue waters of Loch Maree. Gnarled Scots pines on the south bank of the loch make the perfect foreground, while the proud oaks of Letterewe clothe the lower slopes of Slioch, under the buttresses of rich Torridonian sandstone.

Nowadays it is not usually possible to secure a boat to take you across Loch Maree, to make a direct assault on Slioch, but the alternative approach from Kinlochewe is equally delightful.

From the Land Rover track leading to Heights of Kinlochewe, a path branches off to the west and runs along the north bank of the Kinlochewe river. It passes through decayed woods of oak, alder and birch while waves lap the pebbly shore of Loch Maree. Above the path precipitous slopes fall from Meallan Ghobar, and the rock is streaked with foam after a night's rain.

Beinn a'Mhuinidh throws down glistening buttresses into the remarkable rift of Gleann Bianasdail, while the burn (Abhainn an Fhasaigh) roars down a deep ravine which is bridged a short way up from the loch.

Take the path which winds up into Gleann Bianasdail on the west side of the burn, and look out for the herd of wild goats which frequents this rugged and desolate region.

Leave the path at some waterfalls and climb the grassy, ledgy southern slopes of Meall Each to reach a lochan on the bealach under Sgurr Dubh.

The long south-east ridge of Slioch makes a fascinating ascent; two lochans are passed on the shoulder and then steep, bouldery slopes lead to the broad summit where there is a substantial cairn. To the south you can look to Flowerdale and the northern corries of Beinn Eighe; to the north the complex hills and corries of Fisherfield can be seen extending from Beinn Lair to An Teallach while below, Loch Maree with its tree-covered islands runs west for twelve miles. The eastern slopes of Slioch fall into a green, grassy corrie, Coire na Sleaghaich, in which deer can often be seen grazing.

The bare stony ridge curves round to Sgurr an Tuill Bhain and an easy descent into upper Gleann Bianasdail. Cross the burn as it flows into Lochan Fada and walk past several delectable sandy bays at the eastern end of the loch to meet a broad track running back to Kinlochewe. Note that if the exit river from Lochan Fada cannot be easily forded, the only viable alternative is to retrace your steps through Gleann Bianasdail.

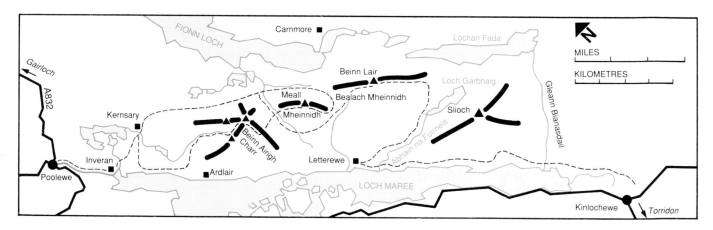

Beinn Airigh Charr 2595ft/791m

Start/Finish: Poolewe (857808)
Map: O.S. 1:50,000 Sheet 19
Distance: 17 miles/27km
Time: 8 hours
Grading: A straightforward ascent of a remote mountain with a long and boggy return march at the end of the day.

Beinn Airigh Charr's pointed summit is prominent from many of the Flowerdale, Torridon and Great Wilderness peaks. It is the most westerly of the long chain of mountains running east–west above the northern shores of Loch Maree: Beinn a'Mhuinidh, Slioch, Beinn Lair, Meall Mheinnidh, Beinn Airigh Charr.

But there is no ferry across Loch Maree and the nearest village, Poolewe, is some way to the west. Thus an ascent of Beinn Airigh Charr is a considerable undertaking. Yet the mountain has the feel of the Great Wilderness about it and such prizes as A'Mhaighdean and Beinn Lair can be clearly seen from its environs.

Notices on the gates near Poolewe make it quite clear that you are not welcome to drive alongside the river Ewe to Inveran or beyond to Kernsary. Never mind, it is an easy and pleasant walk beside the rushing river and through the trees, where we saw siskin, redpoll and a great spotted woodpecker. It is also cheering to read a sign on a gate just before Kernsary saying 'Climbers Welcome'.

As you approach the farm at Kernsary take the rough road that leads south to Ardlair Jetty, but just before the road descends into the trees beside Loch Maree look out for a small cairn on the left. This marks the narrow, but superbly constructed, stalkers' path which makes a rising traverse eastwards into the high west-facing corrie of Beinn Airigh Charr.

The path keeps close to a tumbling burn which in some places is overhung by trees and in others runs through a gorge. On my ascent of this path it was a very wet day and we saw a number of smooth newts and glimpsed two wild goats which loomed out of the mist. The path is still well drained and the tiny streams are bridged by flat stones in a thoroughly professional way. It is extraordinary that they have probably lasted a hundred winters or more.

Finally the path peters out in a shallow green corrie between Spidean nan Clach and Meall Chnaimhean. You should carry on following the stream as it cascades down a rock slab until you reach the grassy bealach between Beinn Airigh Charr and Meall Chnaimhean.

Now head north-east up your main objective; the going is easy and the ground only becomes very steep and rocky just below the pointed summit itself. The O.S. pillar is a round column of concrete and a few other cairns stand nearby. In clear weather you can enjoy wonderful views south across Loch Maree to the Flowerdale Forest and the Torridon hills.

Rather than return to Poolewe the same way, head south for a few hundred metres, then descend east to avoid crags. A long descent takes you down to the quite green Srathan Buidhe under Meall Mheinnidh.

If you have plenty of energy and time left you can easily climb the grassy west ridge of Meall Mheinnidh, avoiding bluffs of rock as they appear. This is another shapely mountain that is an even better viewpoint than Beinn Airigh Charr, particularly across the Dubh Loch to A'Mhaighdean. The south-east slopes lead easily down to Bealach Mheinnidh and the stalkers' path running north to meet the main Carnmore track.

Returning to Srathan Buidhe, the path is regained near a wooden bridge and your return route to Kernsary passes under the superb rock tower of Martha's Peak, the northern outlier of Beinn Airigh Charr.

But this is the only bonus you will receive because the track is abominably wet and boggy, I don't know of a more tiresome and exhausting track anywhere in Scotland. Eventually you arrive at the Kernsary forestry plantation where the path keeps close to the river before breaking out of the trees onto a Land Rover track near Kernsary Farm.

To complete the round trip take the path which traverses above the north shore of Loch Kernsary and leads to the main road not far from the gates of Inverewe Gardens. It is a rather boggy path, not however in the same league as the Kernsary–Carnmore track, but it is preferable to, and a little shorter than, the hard road through Inveran.

Beinn Lair 2822ft/860m

Start: Poolewe (857808)
Finish: Kinlochewe (028619)
Map: O.S. 1:50,000 Sheet 19
Distance: 26 miles/42km
Time: 11–12 hours
Grading: A long, tough walk across a remote and inhospitable region. In winter this expedition should only be attempted by an experienced party.

Walkers on the remote peaks north of the Dubh Loch and Lochan Fada, Beinn a'Chaisgein Mor, A'Mhaighdean and Beinn Tarsuinn marvel at the grand north-facing cliffs which plunge from the summit of Beinn Lair over a distance of two-and-a-half miles.

Beinn Lair is a rewarding but tough objective. It can offer spectacular views over the tree-studded islands of Loch Maree to Beinn Eighe and the Flowerdale Forest, as well as across the wonderfully rugged Fisherfield Forest, but it is extremely remote of access.

Because it is roughly equidistant from Poolewe and Kinlochewe, Beinn Lair's ascent is best included in a long west-east traverse linking the two villages. It would be possible to include the ascent of neighbouring Beinn Airigh Charr and Meall Mheinnidh in this walk, but this would turn this otherwise hugely enjoyable expedition into a marathon and they are best left for another day.

The route into the mountains from Poolewe takes the private road along the north bank of the river Ewe to Inveran. It then bears away north-east to the cottage and loch at Kernsary which is a charming spot ringed with luxuriant gorse, broom, rowan and birch. The surrounding estate was given to the young Osgood MacKenzie, who built Inverewe Gardens, by his father

so the boy could pursue his own sporting interests.

When the path emerges from a small plantation it becomes boggy and rather indistinct, but it never strays far from the Allt na Creige.

Walls and slabs of bare rock descend from the summit of Beinn Airigh Charr and overhang the path. Then you arrive at the deep pass, the Srathan Buidhe, where a choice of route must be made.

You can either take the stalkers' path through the Srathan Buidhe to near Letterewe on Loch Mareeside and then take another path north to Bealach Mheinnidh, a beautiful path with bridges over the burns and tree trunks laid across the boggy sections, or you can continue along the Carnmore path for two miles before turning south to reach the bealach by a steep and winding path.

From Bealach Mheinnidh it is but a short way to the summit plateau of Beinn Lair. Keep to the edge of the cliffs, which can be dramatic in bad weather when the clouds boil like a witch's cauldron and buffets of wind roar and echo around the towers and buttresses sending plumes of vapour racing and swirling up the gullies.

The true summit of Beinn Lair lies back from the cliffs and is marked by a large conical cairn topped with white quartzite. It sits on the wind-scoured plateau strewn with flat slabs of gneiss.

Head east over Sgurr Dubh to two lochans, then descend south down very rough slopes to Loch Garbhaig. In dry weather you can cross the Abhainn na Fuirneis and descend directly to the path alongside Loch Maree, but if this is impossible you must follow the west bank down to the bridge at Furnace.

The Abhainn na Fuirneis foams down to Loch Maree in a series of spectacular waterfalls. In the early eighteenth-century iron ore was smelted with charcoal at Furnace for the manufacture of cannons, and much of the old oak forest was felled. Nevertheless, the oak woods that remain on the north side of Loch Maree are some of the finest in the Highlands.

A delightful switchback path runs through the woods to Kinlochewe. Loch Maree, looking its most majestic, stretches away to the west, waves lap the shores of tiny bays while cascades of water streak down from the upper slopes of Slioch.

A'Mhaighdean 3173ft/967m, Ruadh Stac Mhor 3012ft/918m and Beinn Tarsuinn 3071ft/936m

Start/Finish: Shenavall Bothy (065810)
Map: O.S. 1:50,000 Sheet 19
Distance: 16 miles/25km
Time: 8–9 hours
Grading: These remote mountains in the Great Wilderness are climbed quite easily from an advanced base at Shenavall bothy.

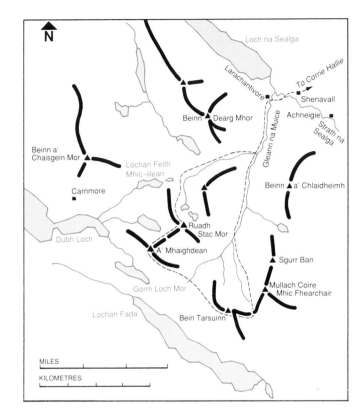

Any mention of A'Mhaighdean puts a gleam in the eye of a Munroist for this wonderful rock peak, set in the heart of the Great Wilderness, is generally recognised to be the most remote Munro and as such is a valuable prize.

A'Mhaighdean is not easily won. I have climbed it both from Kinlochewe and Dundonnell but I cannot honestly recommend these routes because of their exceptionally long approaches. Shenavall bothy makes the most sensible advanced base for A'Mhaighdean, for the neighbouring mountains of Ruadh Stac Mhor and Beinn Tarsuinn can be included in a round of moderate length. If weather, time and fitness allow, the expedition can be extended over Mullach Coire Mhic Fhearchair, Sgurr Ban and Beinn a'Chlaidheimh to complete the classic 'round of the six'.

From Shenavall cross the Abhainn Strath na Sealga and the Abhainn Gleann na Muice and walk up to the watershed near Loch Feith Mhic'-illean, as described in the Corrie Hallie to Poolewe traverse. Easy angled slopes lead up towards Ruadh Stac Mhor but you must pass through a line of broken cliffs to reach the summit.

Weave your way down through steep rocks to the bealach under A'Mhaighdean and then climb easily to the small cairn on the edge of the precipitous south face. You can look straight down to Gorm Loch Mor in its rocky hollow while Lochan Fada stretches away endlessly to the east. On the west side Dubh Loch nestles between dark cliffs.

Gentle, mainly grassy slopes run down to the saddle under Beinn Tarsuinn but then the route dramatically changes charac-

ter. Sandstone bluffs and steps guard the way onto the quite sharp summit ridge of Beinn Tarsuinn which falls away steeply on the north side, enclosing a high corrie with a tiny lochan.

The full extent of Gleann na Muice runs away north for seven miles to the head of Loch na Sealga and An Teallach. From its central position Beinn Tarsuinn provides perhaps the best views of any peak in this guide, with a full 360° panorama of mountains, glens, corries and lochans. Weather permitting, the summit cairn is a place to linger and savour the unique atmosphere of the Great Wilderness.

To return to Shenavall descend easy slopes to the bealach under Meall Garbh, thence down the narrow corrie into Gleann na Muice. In wet weather it is advisable to keep to the east bank of the Abhainn Gleann na Muice for, although this means you forego the stalkers' path on the west side of the glen, it saves at least one potentially tricky river crossing.

Other Worthwhile Routes

1. A'Mhaighdean and Ruadh Stac Mhor can be climbed in a short round from Carnmore, possibly allowing a walk back to Poolewe at the end of the day.

   Leave the Carnmore path above the Dubh Loch and climb up to the tiny Fuar Loch Beag which gives access onto the north-west ridge of A'Mhaighdean. This provides a scrambly route to the summit.

   Return to Carnmore via Ruadh Stac Mhor and Lochan Feith Mhic'-illean where you regain the stalkers' path.

2. Beinn Tarsuinn can be included in the ascent of Mullach Coire Mhic Fhearchair from Kinlochewe.

   From Mullach Coire Mhic Fhearchair retrace your footsteps to the bealach under Meall Garbh and traverse round the north facing slopes to the east ridge of Beinn Tarsuinn.

   Descend the characterful west ridge to the saddle under A'Mhaighdean and then head down rough tussocky slopes to Lochan Fada. Three tiresome miles of trackless and hummocky ground must be traversed to regain the Kinlochewe stalkers' path at the south end of Lochan Fada.

   An alternative, less arduous, return route from Beinn Tarsuinn is to descend the south-east shoulder directly to the end of Lochan Fada. But this avoids the fine ridge running west from the summit which is the mountain's most attractive feature.

Beinn a'Chaisgein Mor 2812ft/857m

> **Start:** *Gruinard Bay (951899)*
> **Finish:** *Poolewe (857808)*
> **Map:** *O.S. 1:50,000 Sheet 19*
> **Distance:** *24 miles/38km*
> **Time:** *10–11 hours*
> **Grading:** *This is a serious expedition to very remote and wild country. Suitable only for fit and experienced walkers.*

Beinn a'Chaisgein Mor is famous for two stupendous cliffs of Lewisian gneiss, Carnmore Crag and Torr na h-Iolaire, which tower above the isolated farm of Carnmore. They provide routes of over 1,000ft in length and are very popular with climbers who are allowed to stay in the stables of the farm by permission of the owner of the Letterewe Estate, on condition that they vacate the premises during the deer stalking season.

Walkers can combine an ascent of Beinn a'Chaisgein Mor with its lowlier neighbour Beinn a'Chaisgein Beag in a long expedition through the incomparable Fisherfield Forest, provided that transport can be arranged at Gruinard Bay or Poolewe. (The bus service is infrequent and the times inconvenient.)

The Gruinard Bay car park is situated beside the bridge carrying the A832 over the Inverianvie river. Take the narrow path which runs along the north bank through an enclosed glen, where at one point the river plunges forty feet over a rock step into a deep pool.

Eventually the path breaks out into an open strath and, near where the river bends abruptly south-west, another grand series of falls and cascades are seen. The path now becomes rather indistinct but it can be followed to the exquisite high Loch a'Mhadaidh which has an island bearing a lone tree and numerous bays and inlets. Keep to the east side of the loch to reach a sandy bay and the Uisge Toll a'Mhadaidh which rushes down a rock gorge into the loch.

The path now disappears completely but the lively river is your guide, leading up through a wide and desolate glen. It is

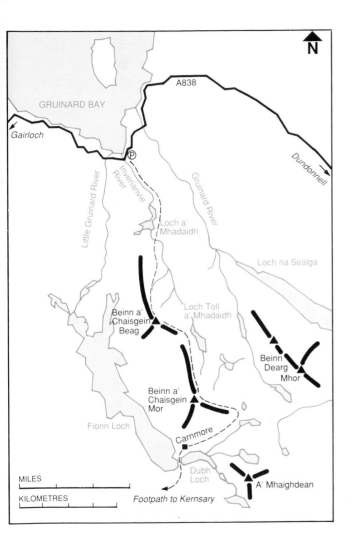

tough going over heather, tussocks and hags. West of the river the bouldery slopes of Beinn a'Chaisgein Beag run down to the glen, and it is easy to climb up to the broad shoulder and follow it south to the main top. You can now look down onto the gloomy Loch Toll a'Mhadaidh circled by broken cliffs, with the saw-toothed ridge of Beinn Dearg Bheag rising behind.

Descend to a saddle and then climb again to a subsidiary summit before reaching the plateau of Beinn a'Chaisgein Mor, from where the line of south-facing crags of A'Mhaighdean are particularly prominent.

In misty weather make sure you head south-east from the summit, rather than south, to avoid the long line of crags overlooking the Dubh Loch. The Shenavall–Carnmore track is met at Loch Feith Mhic'-illean, and this takes you across the Dubh Loch causeway and eventually to Poolewe as described in the Corrie Hallie to Poolewe walk.

Note: It is quite feasible to break this walk by carrying a sleeping bag and staying in the stables at Carnmore Farm, provided this is outside the deer stalking season.

Mullach Coire Mhic Fhearchair 3343ft/1019m, Sgurr Ban 3245ft/989m and Beinn a'Chlaidheimh 3000ft/914m

> *Start:* A832, Loch a'Bhraoin road end (162761)
> *Finish:* Corrie Hallie (114852)
> *Map:* O.S. 1:50,000 Sheet 19
> *Distance:* 22 miles/35km
> *Time:* 11–12 hours
> *Grading:* A long and serious expedition over rough mountain country, involving some rock scrambling and a difficult river crossing towards the end of the day.

Although these hills can be climbed quite easily from a base at Shenavall bothy, my favourite itinerary is from Loch a'Bhraoin to Corrie Hallie. Unfortunately, this necessitates the use of two cars or a hitched lift back to the start at the end of the day. This

expedition involves long but delightful walks to and from the mountains, an ascent of the exposed east ridge of Mullach Coire Mhic Fhearchair and the traverse of Sgurr Ban and Beinn a'Chlaidheimh, two remote Munros in the Great Wilderness.

Leave the A832 at the locked gate near the north end of Loch a'Bhraoin, walk down the track to the boathouse and proceed alongside the loch to the cottage of Lochivraon as described in the Creag Rainich chapter. The cottage used to be homely and clean but it has been badly misused of late and is now decayed, leaking and filled with rubbish.

A path continues up the glen to the ruined bothy of Feinasheen, which sadly can now offer only three walls and some rusty sheets of corrugated iron for shelter. As you round the south shoulder of Creag Rainich a magnificent view unfolds: above Loch an Nid the valley floor widens to give a grassy platform (which makes an ideal camp site), behind rise the bold crags of Tom an Fhiodha which in turn lead to the rock teeth of Sgurr Dubh and a narrow ridge snaking up to the summit of Mullach Coire Mhic Fhearchair. West of Loch an Nid enormous sheets of quartzite slabs, streaked with foaming torrents, run down from the lower slopes of Sgurr Ban, above the east side of the loch tower sandstone cliffs and tree-lined terraces. This is a wild and lonely spot, the haunt of red deer and ravens but rarely visited by humans.

Cross the river near a tumbledown wall and the remnants of a croft and make your way up steep grass, keeping just north of the Tom an Fhiodha cliffs. A break in the cliffs eventually appears and you can scramble up a loose scree slope to the main east ridge of Sgurr Dubh, which has an impressive rock face on the north side.

At the top of Sgurr Dubh the ridge narrows to a razor edge but the sharp flakes of rock can be grasped to enable the considerable degree of exposure to be savoured in safety. This splendid and little known feature of Sgurr Dubh would do justice to the Cuillin. Although this ridge is simple, nervous

Fording the Abhainn Strath na Sealga under the shadow of Beinn Dearg Mhor. Photo: Richard Gibbens.

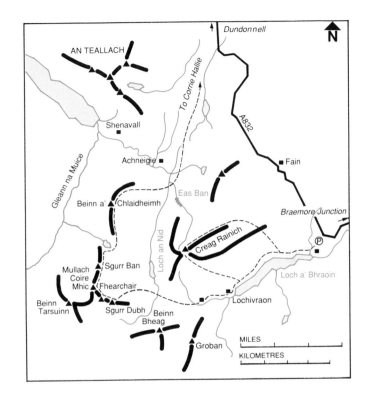

walkers should note that, unlike An Teallach, there is no easy traverse line avoiding the crest.

After a short descent the ridge climbs again in a fine arête to a subsidiary summit with a small cairn. One last heave up the blocks of quartzite and you are at the large cairn and windbreak of the Mullach, surrounded by a wealth of exciting and attractive peaks.

A rather loose, scree-covered ridge takes you north, down to the bealach under Sgurr Ban. Climb easily up Sgurr Ban, a tiresome hill of quartzite carrying an enormous cairn (near which I have seen dotterel) and continue north over the inexorable boulders towards Loch a'Bhrisidh, enjoying wonderful views down to Gleann na Muice and up to Beinn Dearg Mhor and An Teallach. You may notice some strange stone-built igloo-styled shelters near the loch which should be passed on the west side, a less rocky route which provides easier going.

It is a relief to reach the much grassier and quite airy ridge of Beinn a'Chlaidheimh which has several summits. Descend the mountain by its eastern flanks to avoid troublesome crags to the north, although some zig-zagging will still be necessary to reach Strath na Sealga south of Achneigie, near the Eas Ban tributary. The river crossing can be exceedingly troublesome in wet weather. A safety rope should be carried and used without hesitation should the need arise.

Once over the river a broad track leads north to Loch Coire Chaorachain, the wooded Gleann Chaorachain and the car park at Corrie Hallie.

Other Worthwhile Routes

1. Mullach Coire Mhic Fhearchair can be climbed from Kinlochewe but, again, a long approach and return march are involved. Take the private road to the Heights of Kinlochewe and then continue north along a good track to the south-east end of Lochan Fada. Now head due north over rough, rising ground to the shapely outlier of Meall Garbh, thence gain the summit of Mullach Coire Mhic Fhearchair via steep slopes of quartzite boulders.

   A pleasant alternative return route crosses the outflow of Lochan Fada (given reasonably dry conditions) and descends Gleann Bianasdail to the south end of Loch Maree.

   Both routes are 20 miles/32km. Allow 10 hours.

2. The three hills Mullach Coire Mhic Fhearchair, Sgurr Ban and Beinn a'Chlaidheimh can be climbed, together with Beinn Tarsuinn, A'Mhaighdean and Ruadh Stac Mor, in a marathon six Munro round from Shenavall bothy. This

expedition, described in the A'Mhaighdean chapter, is rapidly becoming a classic.

Beinn Dearg Mhor 2986ft/910m and Beinn Dearg Bheag 2690ft/820m

> *Start: Corrie Hallie (114852)*
> *Finish: Gruinard Bay (962912)*
> *Map: O.S. 1:50,000 Sheet 19*
> *Distance: 18 miles/29km*
> *Time: 10–11 hours*
> *Grading: A long expedition over remote and rugged mountains. Some rock scrambling involved and river crossings which could prove troublesome.*

Walkers taking the path from Corrie Hallie to the open bothy of Shenavall, south of An Teallach, gaze with disbelief at Beinn Dearg Mhor when it appears suddenly behind the shoulder of Sail Liath. At only 2986ft/910m, and set amidst the giants of the Fisherfield Forest, it holds the centre of the stage by reason of its craggy north-facing corrie flanked by sharp rocky ridges. The symmetry is perfect and is reminiscent of the north corrie of Ben Lui, except that the scene is grander with deep gullies, seamed buttresses and rock towers. It is often mistaken for An Teallach itself.

Although Shenavall can be used as a convenient base for climbing Beinn Dearg Mhor (outside the deer stalking season) a much finer expedition is to combine its ascent with that of its near neighbour, the illustrious and rarely visited Beinn Dearg Bheag, in an expedition linking Corrie Hallie with Gruinard Bay. Transport must be arranged back to Corrie Hallie at the end of the day.

The stalkers' path from Corrie Hallie leading south into the Great Wilderness is the precursor to many memorable hill days. It climbs up through Gleann Chaorachain to a loch-studded plateau and contours below the rough eastern slopes of An Teallach, where deep heather and slabs of red sandstone lead up to the pinnacles and buttresses of Coire an Lochain.

Opposite Loch Coire Chaorachain a narrow cairned path

branches off to the right, crosses the shoulder of Sail Liath and gradually descends to Shenavall beside a wet gully. The stupendous peak of Beinn Dearg Mhor rises dramatically above the boggy moor directly across Strath na Sealga.

To reach the base of Beinn Dearg Mhor two difficult rivers must be forded and a safety rope should be used if necessary. In wet weather the rivers are unfordable and the whole expedition needs to be reviewed. The first river, Abhainn Strath na Sealga, can be most easily crossed just downstream from Shenavall where it divides round an island. A dreadfully wet stretch of moorland follows before you reach the second river, Abhainn Gleann na Muice. Many maps indicate a bridge over the river but this is false and it must be forded at a point where the river bed is filled with huge boulders just upstream from the locked cottage of Larachantivore.

Follow the path south towards Gleann na Muice Beag for half-a-mile and then start climbing steep heather and rocks to gain the shallow upper corrie of Beinn Dearg Mhor. You should make for the one line of weakness through the protective ring of crags.

At the lip of the upper corrie a stream with waterfalls runs through a rocky gorge caused by landslip. Boulder slopes on the north side of the corrie lead to the eastern summit of the mountain, whence the cliff edge should be followed round to an overhanging rocky prow. The true summit lies on a promontory just beyond the prow where there is a large cairn.

Whatever the conditions this is a thrilling summit. In good weather the view extends south, right across the Great Wilderness with rank after rank of rugged mountains, and when cloudy the mists swirl up between black, dripping cliffs of bare rock, the abyss below your feet seemingly fathomless and like the gateway to hell.

A thousand foot descent of steep, rocky slopes brings you to the bealach under Beinn Dearg Bheag. Below, in a shallow corrie, lies a kidney-shaped lochan and beyond that the grey waters of Loch na Sealga stretch away endlessly on either side.

Beinn Dearg Bheag is a revelation, and it adds an unexpected bonus to the day. Its summit ridge is long and knife-edged, and

it includes four rock turrets. Broken cliffs, blocks and towers of sandstone must be scrambled over in a manner worthy of the Torridonian giants to the south. Scoring poor soil and exposure, tormentil and purple mountain saxifrage thrive between the sandstone rocks.

As you walk west along this exciting ridge you look straight out to the Summer Isles beyond Cailleach Head. Twin-topped Priest Island (Eilean a'Chleirich) is the furthest west of these islands; now uninhabited and a bird sanctuary, it was once the home of the naturalist Fraser Darling, and his life there is fascinatingly described in his book *Island Years*.

Carefully descend the rocky western end of the ridge to the boathouses beside Loch na Sealga. Here you pick up a Land Rover track running for six miles to Gruinard Bay.

Strolling down the long glen makes a pleasant end to the day. The track follows the west bank of the river, passing through

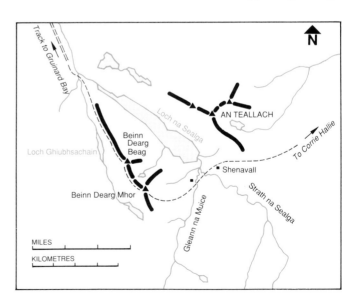

remnants of ancient birch forest and fording the fast flowing tributary, Allt Loch Ghuibhsachain. The Gruinard river has many moods and is always a delight; sparkling over its stony bed, roaring a tempestuous course down cataracts and through ravines, or running deep with its still, black water flecked with foam.

Creag Rainich 2648ft/807m

Start/Finish: A832, Loch a'Bhraoin road end (162761)
Map: O.S. 1:50,000 Sheets 19 and 20
Distance: 11 miles/18km
Time: 6 hours
Grading: An easy mountain walk to a remote and rarely visited summit.

Creag Rainich is the highest point of the huge swelling mass, gently contoured on three sides, which sits squatly between Loch a'Bhraoin and Loch an Nid. It effectively bridges the gap between the illustrious Fannichs and the group of quartzite peaks centred on Mullach Coire Mhic Fhearchair. With the Beinn Dearg hills dominating to the north, Creag Rainich provides a panoramic view of some of the best mountain scenery in the North West Highlands.

In addition, Creag Rainich has a few surprises in store: a succession of sandstone crags fall away precipitously on the west side of the mountain, interspersed with terraces of grass and scrub birch which make popular grazing areas for deer. On the north side, feeder streams from the rather boggy plateau merge to plunge through a wooded gorge, making a splendid waterfall (Eas Ban) before joining the Abhainn Loch an Nid. This spectacular west side of Creag Rainich is the highlight of the Achneigie to Loch an Nid section of the long distance walk from Corrie Hallie to Kinlochewe, which is described at the end of this chapter.

Park in the layby beside the A832 near the Loch a'Bhraoin track. This stretch of the A832 is known as Destitution Road. It was constructed in 1851 as a relief project during the potato famine. Walk down to the boathouse at the north end of the loch

and then follow the path which runs along the west side to the dilapidated cottage of Lochivraon.

This is a delightful path which hugs the water's edge throughout its three mile length. Sometimes you walk on the shingly shore of the loch itself and at other times the path keeps to the turf and heather above the high water mark. There is always plenty of interest: swans, ducks, shags, divers, the wooded slopes of the Fannichs and the view of Slioch away to the south behind the rounded humps of Beinn Bheag and Groban. Halfway along the loch you pass a grassy clearing with ruined crofts and a sheep pen.

Just before Lochivraon cottage make your way up the grassy hillside. There are no paths on Creag Rainich but you can follow an old fence until the angle eases and you reach a tiny lochan under a fringe of crags. The shoulder to the left of the lochan leads to an outcrop of sandstone, the subsidiary summit at 749m.

Descend a short distance to a wide saddle and follow the broad ridge round to the true summit which carries a stone trig pillar. Throughout the ascent your head will be turned aside to admire the rock teeth on the east ridge of Mullach Coire Mhic Fhearchair and the vast, gleaming quartzite slabs descending from Sgurr Ban towards Loch an Nid.

From the summit of Creag Rainich you look north-west beyond the whale-backed Beinn a'Chlaidheimh to the pinnacles of An Teallach, an unforgettable sight on a clear winter's day.

Proceed down the north-east ridge, passing a shallow lochan, and then cross the Allt na Faine which runs down a shallow corrie. Now head for the bealach which leads easily down to the sheep pen near the mid-point of Loch a'Bhraoin.

A view of the stupendous An Teallach ridge from the south showing Corrag Bhuidhe and the pointed peak of Sgurr Fiona. Photo: Jim Teesdale.

An Teallach 3484ft/1062m

Start/Finish: Corrie Hallie (115852)
Map: O.S. 1:50,000 Sheet 19
Distance: 14 miles/22km
Time: 9 hours
Grading: A major mountaineering expedition over one of Britain's finest peaks. The ridge traverse involves some exposed rock scrambling which is suitable for experienced parties only.

From the summits of any of the giant peaks of the far north-west, the Cuillin, Beinn Eighe, Slioch, Sgurr Mor, Beinn Dearg, Ben More Assynt (to name a few), one's gaze is irresistibly attracted to the characteristic cockscomb of An Teallach.

If there is one peak in the Highlands which engenders awe, pumps adrenalin causing the heart to flutter and stirs the emotions, it is An Teallach. I have climbed it many times, yet the anticipation of another ascent still excites me and it has provided some of my greatest ever days in the hills.

An Teallach (the Forge) rises to a height of 3484ft/1062m just south of the head of Little Loch Broom in Wester Ross. The sudden sight of its bare cliffs of red Torridonian sandstone rising into the clouds is almost overwhelming to the driver negotiating the final zig-zag on the descent to Dundonnell from the east.

Why is An Teallach so special? Firstly, the complete traverse is a roller-coaster of a day, a major challenge requiring mountaineering competence and considerable experience. The mountain has a bad accident record and escape from its rocky crest in bad weather is not easy. Secondly, its position commands both the remote, primeval wilderness of the Fisherfield Forest, which has hardly changed since the retreat of the ice-age glaciers 10,000 years ago, and a stretch of wild coastline stretching from Red Point to the Stoer lighthouse. Thirdly, the day's climb includes all the ingredients that go to make up the perfect mountain experience, from a wander through sylvan woods to high, open moorland, exposed scrambling over pinnacles of sound, rough rock and a steep descent of a rugged glen beside a rushing burn to a most welcoming hostelry (the Dundonnell Hotel) on the

shore of a tranquil sea loch.

Park at the Corrie Hallie layby near Dundonnell House and take the stalkers' path running south into the heart of the Fisherfield Forest, a path which is the start of many of Wester Ross's greatest walks. It passes through woods of birch, hazel and alder, with bluebells, violets, wood anemones and wild roses colourful in spring. A burn runs through a gorge beside the path while, beyond, deep heather and slabs of red sandstone lead up to the base of the pinnacles and buttresses of Coire an Lochain. On either side of the corrie, the colossal conical peaks of Glas Mheall Liath and Sail Liath send down wide fans of bruising quartzite screes.

Ford the Allt Chaorachain by stepping stones and zig-zag up to a plateau at 1300ft where a breathtaking panorama of peaks bursts into view: Beinn Dearg and its satellites, the Fannichs, Sgurr Ban, Beinn Tarsuinn, Slioch and Ruadh Stac Mor.

Opposite Loch Coire Chaorachain a narrow cairned path branches off to the right, while the main track continues south to Achneigie. Take this small path which crosses the shoulder of Sail Liath at 1400ft and then gradually descends to Shenavall bothy in Strath na Sealga. At the highest point strike up the broad shoulder of Sail Liath keeping as far as possible to the ridge.

Deep heather and rocks give way to boulder fields of grey quartzite and slabs of sandstone. Because of the wonderful position, particularly the view south to the delightful rocky peak of Beinn Dearg Mhor, a miniature replica of An Teallach itself, the ascent is not too tedious.

I shall never forget the ascent of Sail Liath one unpromising day in late October. There was drizzle and low cloud in Ullapool but, bored by inaction, we donned our wet weather gear and set off up the Achneigie track bound for An Teallach. Half-way up Sail Liath, slipping on the greasy quartzite boulders while freezing mist swirled around, we contemplated cutting our losses and descending to Shenavall bothy to eat our sandwiches and watch the deer. Yet, five minutes later, a watery disc appeared in the sky together with a hint of blue. Almost immediately we broke out above the clouds into warm autumn sunshine.

It was shirt-sleeve order on the 3100ft summit of Sail Liath and

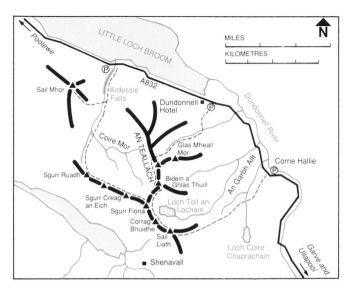

soon as you proceed westwards, down to a bealach and steeply up again to a sharp little peak above Cadha Gobhlach (the forked pass), which sports a new, painstakingly constructed cairn. Then comes another descent to a bealach overlooking Coire Toll an Lochain where, if mist lingers, you may see a Brocken Spectre.

The crux of the An Teallach traverse is the negotiation of the Corrag Bhuidhe pinnacles, the bases of which are reached after a stiff climb. If conditions are bad or if you suffer from vertigo, don't attempt the direct ascent of the pinnacles, but take a narrow sandy path that contours under the rocks on the south side. When difficulties have been by-passed it is an easy, if steep, scramble to regain the crest of the ridge near Sgurr Fiona.

As you approach the Corrag Buidhe pinnacles a 40ft nose of slightly overhanging sandstone blocks your way. But a traverse left and then a steep little wall provide the key to the problem and enable you to reach the crest. This manoeuvre is much easier on the ascent than the descent when, in icy conditions, a rope must be used.

The pinnacles fall away sheer on the north side to the grey waters of Loch Toll an Lochain. Although the position is airy, the rock is sound and the holds are good. In warm weather the traverse of the pinnacles should be savoured. They are much more reminiscent of Arran than the Skye Cuillin because of the rounded, weathered, sandstone. Some pinnacles stand fifteen or twenty feet high either directly on the ridge or slightly detached. You can stand on them to be photographed or sit on them for picnics. They provide an infinite number of bouldering problems of all grades.

One final massive block, overhanging the abyss and known as Lord Berkeley's Seat, is passed before the splendidly pointed summit of Sgurr Fiona is won. Sgurr Fiona was elevated to Munro status by the Brown/Donaldson revision of The Tables in 1981 and no-one could dispute that it is a noble peak and well worth a boost in status. Further, it is interesting to note that Irvine Butterfield has applied the rule of 250ft descent on all sides to the An Teallach massif and has discovered three more possible summits to be added to any entirely objective list of the

we sat blinking beside the cairn while we opened thermos flasks and took in the scene with incredulity. A layer of thick white mist lay over the Highlands to a height of about 2500ft. Only Munros and certain Corbetts emerged above the cotton wool, with their every wrinkle and fissure highlighted by the intense rays of the sun.

Nearby, across Strath na Sealga, towered the perfect horsehoe of Beinn Dearg Mhor with layers of fleecy clouds drifting past its buttresses of black rock. Immediately to the west beckoned the pinnacles of Corrag Bhuidhe, the spire of Sgurr Fiona and An Teallach's main summit, Bidein a'Ghlas Thuill, still streaked with snow. We lingered on Bidein until the sun began to dip over the Minch then, in the gloaming, we raced down through the blanket of freezing mist to Dundonnell for dinner. It had been a day in a million.

Sail Liath is flat topped but the ridge becomes a switchback as

3000-ft peaks. These are Stob Cadha Gobhlach, Glas Mheall Mhor and Sgurr Creag an Eich.

A steep and fairly open descent follows to the curved bealach under Bidein a'Ghlas Thuill. This section of the ridge is particularly prone to icing and may need the use of crampons and ice axe even as late as May.

An Teallach's main top provides the best view of all, back along the ridge with its dripping buttresses plunging northwards to the lochan. West, too, are enchanting views beyond Sail Mhor to the waves racing over the sands of Gruinard Bay, Gruinard Island (now free of anthrax) and the Summer Isles.

A path runs north along the ridge and then descends a loose boulder field to another wide bealach under Glas Mheall Mhor. Cross the low ridge straight ahead by a cairned path and so gain the upper reaches of a long (nameless) glen running down to meet the road one mile north of the Dundonnell Hotel. Long tongues of snow linger in this glen well into spring and facilitate an otherwise rather tiresome descent.

The path follows the line of the burn, first on one side and then on the other, until it passes under fearsome looking boilerplate slabs descending north from Glas Mheall Mhor. At this point cross the burn to the north side and look out for a line of cairns marking the very boggy path which leads down to the main road at the stone-built climbing hut, the Smiddy (JMCS Edinburgh Section).

You are now just 200m from the Dundonnell Hotel or two miles from Corrie Hallie if you wish to return to your car, a lovely walk in spring and early summer with the verges ablaze with rhododendron flowers, a fitting end to one of Britain's most memorable expeditions.

The lost world. Looking east along the An Teallach ridge to Sail Liath and the Fannichs. Photo: Richard Gilbert.

An Teallach By The North-West Ridge

Start/Finish: Ardessie Falls Car Park (052897)
Map: O.S. 1:50,000 Sheet 19
Distance: 14 miles/22km
Time: 8–9 hours
Grading: A remote mountain expedition involving some exposed scrambling. A serious route in winter conditions.

Although the classic traverse of An Teallach is over Sail Liath, Corrag Bhuidhe and Sgurr Fiona, the mountain can be approached from the remote outlier of Sgurr Ruadh giving another magnificent and challenging ridge walk.

Very few walkers brave the tussocky, peat-laden moorlands to climb Sgurr Ruadh and thus gain An Teallach's long north-west ridge. Yet, in spite of very poor weather conditions, I found the route to be full of character and exciting features that were fully in keeping with the standards of this complex and remarkable mountain.

Park at the Ardessie Falls beside Little Loch Broom and take the path uphill on the east side of the burn. At the top of the first rise you can see Sgurr Ruadh rising prominently at the head of a wild and rugged glen down which foams the Allt Airdeasaidh. From this distance a direct ascent of the horrendously steep, rocky nose of Sgurr Ruadh looks impossible but, as you get nearer, the angle eases and you can pick out terraces and gullies.

The path peters out well before you reach Sgurr Ruadh but a reasonable way can be found beside the burn. Once the tributary burn from Lochan Ruadh has been forded the hillside becomes littered with sandstone boulders and it is better drained.

Scramble up the steep rocky slopes just north of the sheer rock nose to reach the first of the twin summits, which has no cairn but gives wonderful views down to Lochan Gaineamhaich and north to Sail Mhor.

Cross to the second peak and begin a long and switchback traverse to Sgurr Creag an Eich. The ridge is rocky and windswept with sandstone tors appearing at intervals, while sheer cliffs overhang Loch na Sealga to the south. Finally, the interminable climb to Sgurr Creag an Eich ends on a sharp and exposed ridge which should be followed eastwards until it dips to a bealach under Sgurr Fiona.

Another steep climb up sandstone boulders, bluffs and turf takes you to the pointed summit of Sgurr Fiona where, if you have previously conquered the main An Teallach traverse, you will be on home ground. Don't relax, as you need to descend steep slopes north from Sgurr Fiona (very icy in winter) before climbing up to the white trig pillar on Bidein a'Ghlas Thuill.

Return to Dundonnell and Ardessie by the wet and rather tedious tourist path described previously.

Other Worthwhile Expeditions on An Teallach

1. From the summit of An Teallach, the sharp east ridge of Bidein a'Ghlas Thuill, which carries sandstone turrets and gendarmes, can be followed to the spur of Glas Mheall Liath. A long and excruciating descent of sharp quartzite scree and loose boulders leads to the stream in Coir' a'Ghiubhsachain, which in turn can be followed, past a waterfall, to the woods beside the A832 a short distance north of Corrie Hallie.

2. If you wish to visit the dramatic amphitheatre of cliffs surrounding Loch Toll an Lochain you can do so by taking the path half a mile north of Corrie Hallie which runs through woods and then follows the approximate line of the stream running down Coir' a'Ghiubhsachain. A succession of sandstone shelves bring you to the water's edge.

   An alternative route takes the track from Corrie Hallie to the junction of the Shenavall path above Loch Coire Chaorachain. From here you should head north-west, taking care when negotiating the descent of a long line of broken cliffs which seemingly bar your way.

   From the loch you can scramble up the scree slopes north of Sail Liath to the low part of the An Teallach ridge at the pass of Cadha Gobhlach, and then continue the high traverse to Bidein a'Ghlas Thuill as described above.

Sail Mhor 2516ft/767m

> *Start/Finish:* A832 at Ardessie Bridge (053896)
> *Map:* O.S. 1:50,000 Sheet 19
> *Distance:* 6 miles/10km
> *Time:* 3–4 hours
> *Grading:* An easy walk beside a series of dramatic waterfalls followed by the ascent of a prominent flat-topped mountain.

This enormously bulky mountain rises like a Christmas pudding from the south shore of Little Loch Broom. It is well worth climbing for the views it provides over the seaboard of Wester Ross and its ascent can be combined with a visit to the spectacular Ardessie Falls.

Park in the layby one mile west of Camusnagaul beside Little Loch Broom. You will see the bridge over the Allt Airdeasaidh with a cascade of white water tumbling over a dark cliff above the road. But this is only one of a succession of splendid falls which are revealed as you climb up the hillside. You pass tree-lined gorges, cataracts and one cirque of sandstone cliffs where the rushing water is split into two streams which plunge headlong into a deep pool.

After about one and a half miles cross the stream and make straight for the south-east ridge of Sail Mhor. This can be climbed easily almost anywhere up grassy slopes which give way to flat sandstone boulders near the top. There is a small cairn at the summit where I once surprised a herd of wild goats with long shaggy hair, horns that swept backwards and billies with beards almost trailing the ground.

Alternative routes of descent are either via the bealach under Ruigh Mheallain on the south side or steeply down from the summit plateau westwards over Sail Bheag.

Beinn Ghobhlach 2083ft/635m

> *Start/Finish:* Allt na h-Airbhe (115931)
> *Map:* O.S. 1:50,000 Sheet 19
> *Distance:* 13 miles/20km
> *Time:* 5–6 hours
> *Grading:* An easy walk to a most attractive, although somewhat isolated, hill.

This prominent twin-topped little peak dominates the peninsula that runs west to Cailleach Head dividing Loch Broom from Little Loch Broom, and it is closely associated with Ullapool. Situated in no-man's-land between Assynt and the Great Wilderness I have placed Beinn Ghobhlach in the latter chapter for convenience.

Many visitors to the bustling west coast fishing port and holiday resort of Ullapool take boat trips to the Summer Isles, to

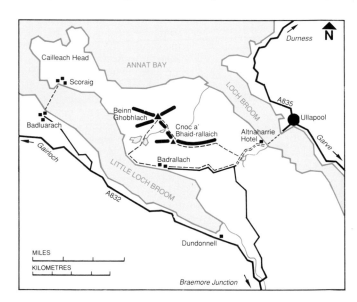

Annat Bay or to the mouth of Loch Broom to watch sea birds and seals and they pass under the Torridonian sandstone cliffs of Beinn Ghobhlach.

It is a hill that is easily climbed and it provides unsurpassed views west over the Summer Isles to the Outer Hebrides and north to the unique mountains of Coigach and Assynt.

By far the most interesting way to approach Beinn Ghobhlach is by ferry from Ullapool to the Altnaharrie Hotel on the south side of Loch Broom. Sadly there is now no regular ferry service but the hotel launch makes several crossings a day and will take passengers from a small fee. Phone 01854 633230.

Once you have disembarked at Altnaharrie you should walk up the rough road to the pass overlooking Little Loch Broom. This point can also be reached by a long drive round via Braemore Junction and Dundonnell where you take the narrow tarmacked road signed to Badrallach.

From the pass strike out westwards over boggy peat, tussocky grass and slightly rising ground to Cnoc a'Bhaid-rallaich where you will be relieved to meet some sandstone outcrops. The knobbly ridge now turns north and descends to the wind ruffled Loch a'Bhealaich which has a beautiful sandy bay on its east side. Scramble quite steeply up to the summit of Beinn Ghobhlach from where a surprisingly steep line of cliffs fall away abruptly to the north. Pause to enjoy the stunning views over the Summer Isles and north beyond the row of white-washed cottages at Achiltibuie to distant Stoer lighthouse.

A more diverse return route descends from Loch a'Bhealaich to the strip of land between Loch a'Coireig and Loch na h-Uidhe, thence down again to meet the path running west above Little Loch Broom to Scoraig.

Scoraig is a remote community accessible only by boat from Badluarach. It has grown steadily over the last twenty years with incoming families renovating ruined cottages and attempting to croft in the traditional way, while others have started craft projects.

The path to Badrallach is a delight; it winds through heather and bracken, often traversing above sandstone cliffs which fall into the loch. You can sometimes see seals on the rocky shore

and gannets diving for fish.

Badrallach is merely a row of cottages, mostly holiday homes, but there is a post box and telephone. Here you meet the road which zig-zags slowly back uphill to meet the Altnaharrie track.

LONG DISTANCE TRAVERSES THROUGH THE GREAT WILDERNESS

By using the network of good stalkers' tracks which run through the Great Wilderness several long distance walks can be enjoyed. These are all demanding expeditions through the wildest mountain country in Britain. There are few emergency shelters and no easy escape routes but these factors make a successful completion particularly satisfying.

North–South Traverse. Corrie Hallie to Kinlochewe

Distance: 21 miles/33km
Time: 9 hours

From Corrie Hallie a rough Land Rover track climbs up through the woods to Loch Coire Chaorachain and then descends in a series of zig-zags to the locked cottage of Achneigie in Strath na Sealga. Leave this track a mile before Achneigie, ford the Eas Ban tributary stream and walk south along the path which runs under the west-facing cliffs of Creag Rainich to Loch an Nid. This point can be reached by an equally pleasant route from the Loch a'Bhraoin road-end, as described in the approach to Mullach Coire Mhic Fhearchair.

Climb up trackless and rather boggy slopes to Bealach na Croise and then descend to the south end of Lochan Fada where an excellent stalkers' path is regained.

From Lochan Fada you must select one of two routes which will take you on to Kinlochewe. Firstly, and more scenically, you can ford the river outflow from Lochan Fada, descend the most attractive Gleann Bianasdail, cross the Abhainn an Fhasaigh by a wooden bridge and return to Kinlochewe by a path through the trees which runs alongside Loch Maree and the Kinlochewe river. Secondly, you can follow the path through Gleann na Muice to pick up the rough road running south through the cottages at the Heights of Kinlochewe to Kinlochewe village itself. For two miles this road follows the Abhainn Bruachaig as it rushes along between banks of gorse and alder while streams cascade down black cliffs on the east side.

An East–West Traverse from Corrie Hallie to Poolewe

> *Distance:* 29 miles/47km
> *Time:* 12 hours

This is one of the great mountain traverses in Britain, considerably rougher, longer and potentially more serious than the Glen Affric traverse or the Lairig Ghru through the Cairngorms. Shelter can be found at Shenavall bothy in Strath na Sealga and at Carnmore at the east end of the Fionn Loch but neither should be used during the deer stalking season. In wet weather, river crossings may be exceedingly troublesome, if not impossible, and a safety rope should be carried and used without hesitation if in doubt.

Start from the layby on the A832 at Corrie Hallie and take the Land Rover track to Achneigie in Strath na Sealga. Continue along the footpath above the river to Shenavall bothy.

Cross the Abhainn Strath na Sealga opposite Shenavall, where it divides round a shingle island, and the Abhainn Gleann na Muice upstream of Larachantivore. Walk up the glen to the conspicuous cliff of Junction Buttress where you should turn off west to Gleann na Muice Beag.

A good stalkers' path climbs to the watershed near Lochan Feith Mhic'-illean and then drops steeply to Carnmore Farm and the Dubh Loch causeway.

As you head west to Kernsary the path runs under the long line of cliffs on Meall Mheinnidh and Beinn Airigh Charr. Note that in wet weather the Abhainn Srathan Buidhe is bridged 300m

upstream of the ford.

A boggy stretch follows to the Kernsary plantation, but at the loch you leave the mountains behind and can enjoy a pleasant stroll along the rough road to Inveran and then beside the river Ewe into Poolewe.

Other Worthwhile Low Level Walks

1. A Visit to Shenavall Bothy in Strath na Sealga

> *Distance:* 13 miles/21km
> *Time:* 6 hours

From the layby at Corrie Hallie take the track south to near Loch Coire Chaorachain. Where the path divides (small cairn) take the right-hand branch which leads over the lower shoulder of Sail Liath and then descends beside a wet gully to Shenavall.

Enjoy the view of Beinn Dearg Mhor, walk to the end of Loch na Sealga and watch out for deer grazing beside the river.

Walk up the Strath to the private cottage of Achneigie which is set among trees and return to Corrie Hallie via the track which zig-zags up the hill to Loch Coire Chaorachain and descends once more to Corrie Hallie.

2. A Walk Alongside Loch na Sealga to Gruinard Bay

> *Distance:* 16 miles/25km
> *Time:* 8 hours

Transport is required from Gruinard Bay to Corrie Hallie at the end of the day. Do not attempt this walk in wet weather, unless you are prepared to carry a safety rope, because of dangerous river crossings.

From Corrie Hallie walk to Shenavall bothy as described above. Ford the Abhainn Strath na Sealga and cross the flat,

boggy moorland to Larachantivore. Now ford the Abhainn Gleann na Muice to reach the path on the west side of Loch na Sealga.

After a short distance the path peters out but it is easy to follow the stony shore of the loch or the hummocky ground just above the high water mark.

At the north end of the loch, at a boathouse, you meet an excellent Land Rover track which meanders very pleasantly beside the river for six miles to Gruinard Bay.

3. Loch a'Bhraoin to Corrie Hallie via Loch an Nid

> *Distance:* 15 miles/24km
> *Time:* 8 hours

This superb walk takes you easily into the Great Wilderness where you can appreciate, at close quarters, the east ridge of Mullach Coire Mhic Fhearchair, Beinn Dearg Mhor and the relentless southern slopes of An Teallach.

From the A832 walk down to the boathouse beside Loch a'Bhraoin and then continue south alongside the shore to Lochivraon cottage. Continue up the glen to the ruined bothy of Feinasheen, round the shoulder of Creag Rainich and descend to Loch an Nid.

Continue walking north down this enchanting glen, ford the tributary stream coming from the Eas Ban waterfall, and meet the Achneigie to Corrie Hallie track.

A view east from Beinn Airigh Charr. Left to right: A'Mhaighdean, Mullach Coire Mhic Fhearchair and Beinn Tarsuinn. Photo: Stephen Greenwood.

6 THE FANNICHS

The Fannichs are a splendidly compact group of mountains which have the reputation of being easy, rounded and grassy, rather like the northern Pennines or the Howgills. This impression is confirmed by the limited view obtained of them from the A835 when driving westwards from Loch Glascarnoch.

Yet this does the Fannichs an injustice for there are many fine corries and steep rock faces to be found in the heart of the range. Winter climbing is developing rapidly. There are ten separate Munros to be climbed and, in the aloof and pointed summit of Sgurr Mor 3637ft/1110m, we have the highest hill in Scotland north of Glen Affric's Carn Eige. In addition, walkers on holiday in North West Scotland who have been bruised by the relentless quartzite screes of Sgurr Ban, An Teallach and Ben More Assynt, or exhausted by the ever deteriorating bogs on the Carnmore track, may welcome a change to easier terrain.

Although it is possible to traverse the entire range from east to west in a day, it is much more enjoyable to take the hills section by section in a more relaxed fashion. Thus I have divided the Fannichs into four separate expeditions, excluding the outlying peak of Fionn Bheinn above Achnasheen which can be climbed in a few hours.

Since it is no longer possible to obtain keys to the locked gates on the road running from Lochluichart to Fannich Lodge, easy access to the Fannichs is limited to the A835 and the Loch a'Bhraoin approach from the north and west.

October mist in the Fannichs. Sgurr Mor from Beinn Liath Mhor Fannaich. Photo: Richard Gilbert.

Fionn Bheinn 3061ft/933m

Start/Finish: Achnasheen (164586)
Maps: O.S. 1:50,000 Sheets 20 and 25
Distance: 6 miles/10km
Time: 4–5 hours
Grading: A simple half-day's excursion up a very accessible Munro.

This isolated wedge shaped mountain has smoothly contoured convex slopes running down to Achnasheen, and its appearance hardly sets the pulse racing. But when seen across Loch Fannich from Sgurr nan Each or Meall Gorm its rocky upper corrie, Toll Mor, gives it some stature and dignity.

Fionn Bheinn can be climbed easily in a few hours from Achnasheen. Directly opposite the hotel a track by-passes a group of buildings and runs uphill to meet the banks of the Allt Achadh na Sine; an indistinct path can then be followed for a short distance until it peters out.

The burn makes a useful feature to follow as you climb boggy hillside to the bealach east of Fionn Beinn's summnit and then hug the edge of the Toll Mor corrie to the stark concrete trig pillar. The view south-east is to the shapely and intriguing group of hills north of Strathconon which include the Corbetts of Meallan nan Uan and Sgurr a'Mhuilinn.

You can either return the same way or deviate slightly east to the shoulder of Creagan nan Laogh before making the descent to the low ground.

Beinn Liath Mhor a'Ghiubhais Li 2513ft/766m

Start/Finish: Bridge over Abhainn an Torrain Duibh (277742)
Map: O.S. 1:50,000 Sheet 20
Distance: 7 miles/11km
Time: 4 hours
Grading: An easy walk up a rounded and grassy hill.

Beinn Liath Mhor a'Ghiubhais Li is a rather nondescript and featureless Corbett which rises in a smooth dome just south of Loch Glascarnoch. A little character is given by tongues of grey boulder scree which run some way down the slopes from the summit.

The hill could be very quickly ascended from the A835 but a more worthwhile round is to approach from the south. Take the path along the west bank of the Abhainn an Torrain Duibh for three miles until you reach a wooden bridge. Cross the bridge and climb the rough slopes beyond until the deep heather gives way to easier wind-scoured ground. (You may notice a stalkers' shelter constructed of dry stones.)

From this subsidiary hill head north to Beinn Liath Mhor a'Ghiubhais Li which is an excellent viewpoint south to An Coileachan, Meall Gorm and Sgurr Mor and, more particularly, north to Am Faochagach, Cona Mheall and Beinn Dearg.

Descend northwards beside a new forestry plantation to reach the road.

Meall Gorm 3114ft/949m and An Coileachan 3028ft/923m

Start/Finish: Bridge over Abhainn an Torrain Duibh (277742)
Map: O.S. 1:50,000 Sheet 20
Distance: 13 miles/20km
Time: 6–7 hours
Grading: A long expedition to two rounded hills involving a tough approach through heather and coarse grass.

The saving grace of these two rather lumpy hills is the cliff-girt Garbh Choire Mor on the east ridge of An Coileachan. This can be visited easily from the private road that runs south of the range to Fannich Lodge but unfortunately it is well off route when the hills are approached from the north.

Park beside the bridge over the Abhainn an Torrain Duibh, where there is a convenient layby, and take the path on the west side of the river for about three miles until you reach a footbridge over the Abhainn a'Ghiubhais Li at a height of 1250ft/380m. Cross the river and climb rough slopes of deep heather, peat hags, hidden boulders and hummocky moraines to the mound of Meallan Buidhe, whence a short descent takes you to the bealach between Loch Gorm and Loch nan Eun.

Straight ahead lies the saddle between An Coileachan and Meall Gorm, but you can climb steep slopes to the left leading directly to the summit of An Coileachan. The going gets much easier above 2500ft/800m, when the heather and hags are left behind to be replaced by stony, wind-scoured ground.

Excellent walking over open, bouldery slopes leads north-west to Meall Gorm. Just past a false summit which bears a small cairn you will notice a strange stone-built shelter erected for stalkers.

From Meall Gorm summit strong walkers can continue to head north-west, over the intermediate top of Meall nam Peithirean, to gain Sgurr Mor, returning to the road via Beinn Liath Mhor Fannaich, but I recommend leaving these summits for another day.

To regain the car park follow the north-west ridge of Meall Gorm down to the bealach under Meall nam Peithirean and descend further to the outflow of Loch an Fhuar Thuill Mhoir. You now have a long haul back, five miles via Loch Li, the Abhainn a'Ghiubhais Li and the Abhainn an Torrain Duibh, to the bridge.

Beinn Liath Mhor Fannaich, 3130ft/954m, and Sgurr Mor 3642ft/1110m

Start/Finish: *Loch Droma dam (253755)*
Map: *O.S. 1:50,000 Sheet 20*
Distance: *10 miles/16km*
Time: *6 hours*
Grading: *An easy and enjoyable ascent of the highest mountain in northern Scotland.*

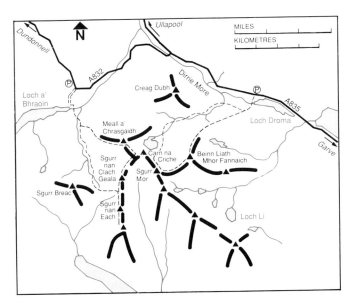

Park at Lochdrum at the north end of Loch Droma, which is a most attractive loch fringed with pine trees making the ideal foreground for views of An Teallach when driving west across the Dirrie More.

Cross the dam and take the Water Board's rough access road as it climbs gently up the glen to a subsidiary dam at the end of a pipeline. Although the map shows the road ending at this point it has now been bulldozed for a further mile, ending at a turning place.

Leave the access road at the subsidiary dam where there is a vegetated gorge and take to the hillside which is grassy and not too steep. Make a rising traverse to gain the north ridge of Beinn Liath Mhor Fannaich which leads directly to the summit itself. I have happy memories of this mountain: it was once so still that we lit a stove and boiled a kettle for tea by the cairn, and on another occasion, in October, we experienced inversion with just the highest tops, Sgurr Mor, Beinn Dearg and An Teallach visible above a sea of cotton wool cloud.

Rather bleak exposed slopes of moss, grass and flat stones lead round the corrie to Sgurr Mor. The last few hundred feet are quite steep and if you keep to the north-facing escarpment you can enjoy a degree of exposure. This high corrie face of Sgurr Mor has yielded some top quality winter climbs.

There is a large, well built cairn on Sgurr Mor befitting such a shapely peak and fine viewpoint from where I have seen the hills of Harris rising way beyond the Summer Isles in the mouth of Loch Broom. If the weather is kind you should sit by the cairn on Sgurr Mor, open the thermos flask and enjoy the view. To the north, behind the grassy dome of Beinn Enaiglair, rise the Beinn Dearg hills, further west you can identify the shapely hills of Coigach and Assynt while south and west your eyes will be drawn to the sharp dragon's teeth on An Teallach, the remote

Fannaich, Sgurr Mor, Sgurr nan Clach Geala and Sgurr nan Each. But they had great difficulty in fording the burn and became benighted.

For light they had precisely three matches. The first showed the map to be folded upside down, the second blew out and the third gave them insufficient information. After freezing and blundering about all night they reached the road at 7.00am to find Munro's driver still waiting with the dog cart, with a fire alight and hot cocoa ready.

High summer on the broad north-west ridge of Beinn Dearg. Photo: Richard Gilbert.

7 THE BEINN DEARG FOREST

I have given this name to the huge area of attractive mountains and glens which comprise the deer forests of Inverlael, Freevater, Braemore and Strathvaich. It extends from the A835 and the Glascarnoch reservoir in the south as far north as the A837 and the river Oykel.

The mountains are bulky with rounded shoulders of coarse grass while glaciation has produced many steep and cliff-girt north facing corries which hold snow well into early summer. Many of the hills have flattish boulder strewn plateaux which overlook deep glens and provide homes for mountain hares and ptarmigan.

Fortunately there are no motorable roads or tracks through this wild area and, when on the hills, you experience an overwhelming sense of loneliness. Outside the deer stalking season there are no permanent habitations except on the periphery but two open bothies, Glenbeg cottage and Coiremor bothy, would provide emergency shelter.

The Beinn Dearg Forest contains two of the finest Munros in northern Scotland: Beinn Dearg itself and the very remote and highly prized Seana Bhraigh. Strong walkers should place these hills high up on their list of objectives.

The character of the Beinn Dearg hills is close to that of the big ranges in western Scotland: the hills of Glens Affric, Cannich and Strathfarrar and the neighbouring Fannichs. South lie the great sandstone/quartzite peaks of Torridon and north lie the individual monoliths of Coigach and Assynt, the bare Lewisian gneiss peaks of Glencoul and the distinctive quartzite hills of Conival, Ben More Assynt and the Reay Forest.

Beinn Enaiglair 2917ft/889m

Start/Finish: Braemore Junction (208777)
Map: O.S. 1:50,000 Sheet 20
Distance: 7 miles/11km
Time: 4–5 hours
Grading: A varied and easy walk up a mainly grassy hill which is an outstanding viewpoint.

Beinn Enaiglair is the prominent hump which rises west of Beinn Dearg. When seen down the length of Loch Broom from Ullapool it is often mistaken for Beinn Dearg itself.

Although it can be climbed with Beinn Dearg in an expedition from Inverlael or Braemore Junction, Beinn Enaiglair does not naturally fit into any of the Beinn Dearg circuits described in this chapter and it makes a pleasant, albeit modest, expedition in its own right. The hill stands off from the Fannichs and gives the best view of all of this compact range.

Park at Braemore Junction and take the gated estate road through the forest to the site of the old shooting lodge. At a low stone-built cottage a track zig-zags through the rhododendrons, heading up the hillside towards Home Loch. On my most recent visit a water pipe had just been buried beside the track which had been bulldozed into quagmire.

Home Loch is a lonely sheet of water with a picturesque boatshed and a single pine tree standing on the shore. The stalkers' path runs up the hillside to the bealach between Beinn Enaiglair and Meall Doire Faid, but at an ancient dry-stone sheep pen take the path branching due north which takes you to the broad west ridge of Beinn Enaiglair. Climb the heathery slopes to the flattish top of the mountain, where I once surprised a herd of seventy deer grazing an area of deep moss.

If you are continuing to Beinn Dearg don't attempt to descend the north-east ridge straight from the summit cairn. There are crags. Instead, descend the south-east ridge for a short distance and then cut back under the crags to the bealach. The round hill Iorguill 2861ft/872m leads easily to the main north-west ridge of Beinn Dearg described elsewhere.

To return to Braemore descend easy slopes south to the bealach under Meall Doire Faid where you pick up the good path to Home Loch.

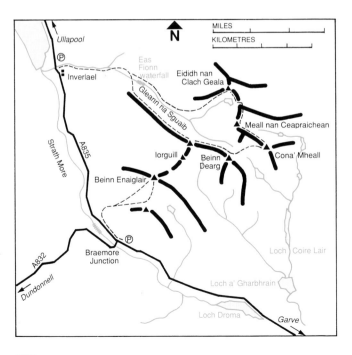

Coast To Coast In A Day
Inverlael to Bonar Bridge

Start: Inverlael (182853)
Finish: Ardgay (590892)
Maps: O.S. 1:50,000 Sheets 20 and 21
Distance: 33 miles/53km
Time: 12–14 hours
Grading: A very long walk through lonely and uninhabited glens. River crossings could be difficult in wet weather.

The ascent of mountains is not the only objective for a day's walking in Scotland. What could be more challenging than a walk right across Scotland from coast to coast? The narrowest neck of land lies between the east end of Loch Broom and the west end of the Dornoch Firth; the crossing is not too arduous for a fit party, the route is diverse, the scenery entrancing and the completion immensely satisfying.

Set out early from the seaweedy shores of Loch Broom and cross the road to Inverlael. Now take the road through the forest into beautiful Gleann na Sguaib and follow the path beside the tumbling river to the group of tiny lochans at the bealach under the vast bulk of Beinn Dearg.

Pick your way down moraines to Loch Tuath, a remote and shallow loch decorated with reeds and water lilies. The loch is enclosed by great slabs of grey rock rising to the summit of Cnap Coire Loch Tuath on the north side, while Cona' Mheall seals it off from the south.

Continue past Loch Prille, cross a tiresome area of black peat, and drop down to the broad strath of Gleann Beag, with the rocky turrets of Seana Bhraigh just appearing over the ridge.

Make for the open bothy of Glenbeg Cottage and then pass under the rugged, splintered cliffs of Carn Loch Sruban Mora. Soon afterwards the merry burn is chanelled off into pipes, and a Land Rover track leads down the glen to the prosperous, white-washed Deanich Lodge.

A long six-mile stretch of track through Gleann Mor lies ahead but, near Alladale Lodge, the bare hillsides sprout birch

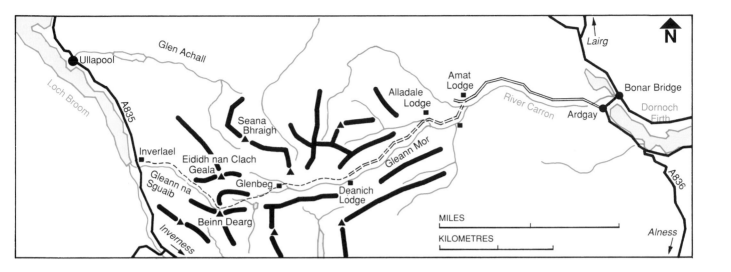

and willow, the river enters a gorge and the path twists through bracken, foxgloves and Caledonian pines.

You pick up a tarmac road at Glencalvie Lodge and this runs north to a magnificent stand of pine, spruce, beech, oak and Wellingtonia trees in the grounds of Amat Lodge. The road follows the turbulent river Carron for ten miles, until it meets the Dornoch Firth at Ardgay.

A Round of the Beinn Dearg Hills: Eididh nan Clach Geala 3045ft/928m, Meall nan Ceapraichean 3205ft/977m, Cona' Mheall 3215ft/980m and Beinn Dearg 3,556ft/1,084m

Start/Finish: Inverlael (182853)
Map: O.S. 1:50,000 Sheet 20
Distance: 16 miles/26km
Time: 9 hours
Grading: A long and rather complex circuit of a group of fine peaks. Route finding could be a problem in bad weather.

Driving over the Dirrie More at the west end of Loch Glascarnoch the road runs between two superb ranges of high mountains: the Fannichs and the Beinn Dearg hills. The ranges are quite similar in form because both are composed of Moine schists. Just a hint of the east facing cliffs of Beinn Dearg can be seen from Glascarnoch whereas from Ullapool its great triangular shaped northern rock face is very prominent.

Beinn Dearg and its three satellite Munros are best climbed from Inverlael on the north-west side because the approach from the south involves an exasperating walk across an area of hideous peat-hags and bogs.

Park near the forest gate at Inverlael and walk up the rough road through the trees into Glenn na Sguaib. This is a typically romantic Scottish glen: a swift river tumbles down in a series of cascades and falls, running in places through deep dark gorges while the south side of the glen is bounded by broken cliffs, overgrown with birch and rowan.

Just beyond the Eas Fionn waterfall the path branches, marked by a cairn, and you should take the left hand branch which runs high onto the west ridge of Eididh nan Clach Geala. After passing a few shallow lochans follow a rocky mound to the summit where there are several enormous blocks of white quartzite (the name Eididh nan Clach Geala means Web of the White Stones).

The saving grace of this rather low and accessible Munro is a line of crags on the side overlooking Lochan a'Chnapaich. You should follow the line of these crags to gain the bealach under Meall nan Ceapraichean and then tackle the steep slopes above, threading your way through rocky bluffs to reach the stony upper plateau of this mountain. Enjoy a close up view of the north face of Beinn Dearg which holds snow patches well into the summer.

Descend again to a lochan under Cona' Mheall and then climb to another tiny lochan on the ridge which is adjacent to a substantial boundary wall. This lochan has steeply shelving sides and makes an ideal spot for a dip on a hot summer's day. If you are carrying heavy rucksacks leave them here for collection on your return from making a detour to the summit of Cona' Mheall.

Cona' Mheall is a most shapely peak with towering cliffs on the south side overlooking Loch a'Choire Ghranda, which is bounded on the west side by Beinn Dearg's equally precipitous east face.

Retrace your footsteps to the lochan and follow the line of the wall onto the upper slopes of Beinn Dearg. This wall is an impressive feature which runs for miles down towards Inverlael from Beinn Dearg's summit. Vast slabby boulders have been laid horizontally to form a base on which other slabs have been set vertically. At intervals huge stone pillars key the wall. The boulders used are so enormous that you feel the wall must surely have been built by giants! Today it is virtually undamaged.

The massive summit cairn of Beinn Dearg is set about 200ft above the line of the wall. It is a wonderful viewpoint with Seana Bhraigh, Ben Hope, Ben Wyvis, An Teallach and the hills of the Fannichs and Torridon clearly visible.

Follow the wall down the wide and undulating west ridge until it ends abruptly at a cairn one mile short of Inverlael Forest. Descend steepish heather and grass to Gleann na Sguaib.

Other Worthwhile Routes

1. Descend the very narrow and rocky south ridge of Cona' Mheall to Loch Coire Lair and cross the bogs and peat-hags surrounding Loch a'Gharbhrain to meet the A835 road at the west end of Loch Glascarnoch.

2. Deviate from the descent of the west ridge of Beinn Dearg to the grassy hill of Iorguill, thence climb Beinn Enaiglair. Descend further to the bealach under Meall Doire Faid and pick up the stalkers' path leading to Home Loch and Braemore Junction.

Am Faochagach 3130ft/954m

Start/Finish: Bridge over Abhainn an Torrain Duibh (277742)
Map: O.S. 1:50,000 Sheet 20
Distance: 10 miles/16km
Time: 6–7 hours
Grading: A difficult and tiring approach but the mountain has a long and high summit ridge that gives magnificent walking.

In appearance Am Faochagach is one of the most featureless of the Ross-shire Munros, yet in winter I have enjoyed the most exhilarating of days tramping across level frozen snow on its broad summit ridge, blue sky overhead, not a breath of wind and with magnificent views extending to far horizons.

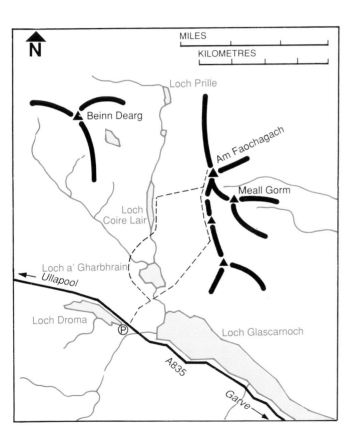

The usual route of ascent is from the bridge over the Abhainn an Torrain Duibh at the north end of Loch Glascarnoch. Cross rough hillocks to the bank of the Abhainn a'Gharbhrain and carefully ford this rushing river. In dry weather you can boulder-hop. In normal conditions you must wade (up to knee deep) but when the river is in spate you must use a safety rope or else look for another objective.

A deer path climbs the hillside beside the Allt na h-Uidhe and when it peters out you should continue up the heathery slopes to the rounded, undulating north ridge of Am Faochagach. After two miles and several false summits you reach the cairn from where you can enjoy a birds-eye-view into Choire Ghranda between Beinn Dearg and Cona' Mheall and over the rarely visited hills of the Tollomuick and Inchbae Forests.

Retrace your steps for a short distance and then descend easy grass slopes and boulder fields to the shore of tranquil Loch Coire Lair. On my last visit we sat and ate our sandwiches one hundred feet above the loch, watching entranced as an otter swam and played in the mirror-calm water.

When returning to the road from Loch Coire Lair it is preferable to head west of Loch Gharbhrain, crossing both the out-flowing burn of Loch Coire Lair and the Allt a'Gharbhrain. A small patch of grass and some tumbled down walls indicate the site of an old crofting settlement, but there is no path and the going is extremely tiresome over deep black bogs and peat hags.

Other Worthwhile Routes

1. Am Faochagach can be climbed easily from the east by walking up the rough road to the dam at the southern end of Loch Vaich. Make your way a short distance along the lochside, cross the Allt Glas Toll Mor and ascend the long south-east ridge of Am Faochagach over Meall Gorm.

2. A pleasant circuit of Am Faochagach, Cona' Mheall and Beinn Dearg can be made from the Abhainn an Torrain Duibh bridge. Follow the Allt a'Gharbhrain upstream for a mile from Loch a'Gharbhrain and climb Beinn Dearg by its huge and gently angled south shoulder. The famous wall,

described above in the Beinn Dearg chapter, guides you down to the bealach and lochan under Cona' Mheall, which is then climbed by its stony west ridge. Now descend the exciting south ridge of Cona' Mheall, on the north side of Choire Ghranda, to the Allt Lair immediately under the summit of Am Faochagach. Pick the easiest way up the 2000ft of steep grass to reach the summit and return to the road by the route of ascent described above.

Seana Bhraigh 3041ft/927m

> *Maps: O.S. 1:50,000 Sheets 20 and 16*

Although the main cluster of peaks making up the Beinn Dearg Forest is reasonably accessible from the south, the northern outlier, Seana Bhraigh, is distinctly remote and is highly prized by the Munroist. Seana Bhraigh lies in a desolate and craggy region of the Northern Highlands, amongst steeply convoluted mountains and unspoilt glens, and there is no easy route of approach. Each of the three routes described below give splendidly long hills days, guaranteed to stretch the legs and clear the cobwebs, but it is worth noting that only the first of these returns you to your starting point. The others require more detailed transport arrangements.

Seana Bhraigh via Glen Achall

> *Start/Finish: Glen Achall (147955)*
> *Distance: 26 miles*
> *Time: 12 hours*
> *Grading: A long and arduous day although much of the route to and from the mountain is along a good track.*

From Ullapool drive along the rough road into Glen Achall and park just beyond the quarry. You now have a seven mile walk along a Land Rover track above the Rhidorroch River but there is plenty of interest with the shoreline of Loch Achall and then a line of imposing cliffs above East Rhidorroch Lodge.

Where the river turns sharply to the south and becomes the river Douchary leave the track and descend a gorge through damp woods before climbing again into Glen Douchary. The river Douchary has carved out a series of magnificent cascades and waterfalls from the bedrock; one is particularly memorable with a sheet of water falling 100ft sheer into an amphitheatre, at the bottom of which stands a huge pointed boulder carrying a Caledonian pine tree.

Skirt Meall nam Bradhan and climb the broad grassy slopes of the north-west shoulder of Seana Bhraigh directly to the summit. From the stumpy O.S. pillar, which is surrounded by a low circular wall of boulders, the big northern corric falls right away in vegetated cliffs to Loch Luchd Choire nearly 1500ft below.

The loch is enclosed by a cirque of cliffs rising on the north side of An Sgurr, a subsidiary summit of spiky rock on the northern side of Creag an Duine.

A pleasant variation on the return march is to walk over the grassy hills of Meall nam Bradhan to Lochan Badan Glasliath and then enter the impressive ravine of the Allt nan Caorach which is deep, narrow and rocky. A lonely and fascinating place! Once through the ravine you soon regain the Glen Achall track.

Seana Bhraigh via Glen Achall and Strath Nimhe

> *Start: Glen Achall (147955)*
> *Finish: Leckmelm (168901)*
> *Distance: 21 miles*
> *Time: 10 hours*
> *Grading: Similar to the previous route but a slightly shorter return.*

This route climbs Seana Bhraigh via the Glen Achall/Glen Douchary route described above but returns to the road a shorter way, meeting the A835 at Leckmelm.

Descend the north-west shoulder of Seanna Bhraigh to Glen Douchary, and at the junction of the river with Allt Siolar traverse westwards through heather and over rough tussocks to meet the stalkers' track in Strath Nimhe. This leads down beside an area of new forestry to Leckmelm.

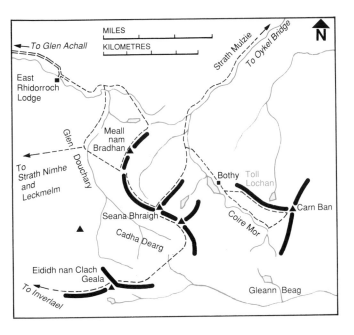

Seana Bhraigh. A Crossing from Inverlael to Oykel Bridge

Start: Inverlael (182853)
Finish: Oykel Bridge (385009)
Distance: 23 miles
Time: 11–12 hours
Grading: A long and serious expedition but it provides the perfect combination of hill, crag and glen.

This route takes on Seana Bhraigh directly. It is a serious expedition and there are no escape routes but it is the most satisfying

way of climbing the mountain.

Park at Inverlael and take the path through the forest into Gleann na Sguaib. At the Eas Fionn waterfall strike up Eididh nan Clach Geala as described for the Beinn Dearg circuit.

Head north from the summit of Eididh nan Clach Geala, over steep slopes of slippery lichen-encrusted boulders, and then make for the west-facing crags of Seana Bhraigh which can be seen across a desolate wasteland of bogs, burns, peat-hags, lochans, hillocks and crags.

On the north side of the plateau the ground falls away precipitously to Cadha Dearg, the corrie of upper Glen Douchary, and the most interesting traverse route follows the lip of the cliff. To the south, rough boggy ground, interspersed with rock outcrops, gradually falls away to Gleann Beag which drains into the Dornoch Firth at Bonar Bridge. Since the Douchary river runs into the Atlantic ocean the plateau is a true watershed of Scotland.

Seana Bhraigh throws down wet, mossy cliffs into Cadha Dearg. Streams cascade down these cliffs which are composed of seamed and shattered schists producing terraces, chasms and fissures, but they are easily skirted on the east to gain the summit of the mountain.

Descend Seana Bhraigh in a northerly direction, passing a tiny lochan on the ridge. The full extent of Strath Mulzie can be seen running away into the far distance, eight miles to the forestry plantation below Duag Bridge. Four miles beyond Duag Bridge stands the Oykel Bridge Hotel, a haven of civilisation and comfort at the end of the walk.

Strath Mulzie is wide and desolate, only narrowing at the upper end where Loch a'Choire Mhoir is enclosed between craggy slopes. The north ridge of Seana Bhaigh allows an enticing peep into the upper corrie where the lonely grey-stone cottage of Coiremor sits beside the loch. Coiremor is an open bothy maintained by the Mountain Bothies Association.

A good track runs down Strath Mulzie but in wet weather the fording of the Allt a'Choire Bhuidhe could be a problem. At Corriemulzie Lodge you pass through a collection of white-washed buildings and then the glen becomes more enclosed;

birch, hazel and rowan grow on the banks and ravines have been carved through the rock.

On the hillside above Duag Bridge considerable areas of ancient birch forest are thriving. They provide an essential ingredient to this very beautiful and very Scottish scene. This is more than can be said for the square blocks of fir plantations that begin just below Duag Bridge and continue almost to the road at Oykel Bridge.

Carn Ban 2772ft/845m

Start/Finish: Coiremor bothy (305887)
Map: O.S. 1:50,000 Sheet 20
Distance: 5 miles/8 km
Time: 4 hours
Grading: The ascent of a remote and featureless mountain is simplified by spending a night at Coiremor bothy.

Carn Ban is a tough but thoroughly worthwhile objective because it takes you into the heart of the Freevater Forest. This vast area of rolling hills, very long glens and salmon rivers is without habitation, save for a few shooting lodges, and it teems with deer whose sheer numbers have become an embarrassment to the landowners.

The ascent of Carn Ban could be combined with that of Seana Bhraigh by any of the routes already described but this would make such an exceptionally long day that I cannot recommend it. However, a comfortable open bothy maintained by the Mountain Bothies Association is situated in a truly superb position on the shore of Loch a'Choire Mhoir. This can be used to make a much more leisurely ascent of Carn Ban.

Coiremor bothy is tucked under the north-west ridge of Carn Ban and it looks across the loch to the towering north-facing cliffs of Seana Bhraigh. On my most recent visit in late October four whooper swans were resting on the loch, salmon were leaping from the water and stags were roaring in the corries of Seana Bhraigh. The evening was dark and chilly but we found plenty of bogwood for the stove in the peat hags at the end of the loch.

The approach to Coiremor from the north involves a twelve-mile walk from Oykel Bridge via the forestry road to Duag Bridge and the track through Strath Mulzie. But outside the stalking season permission can sometimes be given for a car to be driven as far as Corriemulzie Lodge, saving half the walk. Enquire at the Oykel Bridge Hotel.

Easy grassy slopes rise from behind the bothy to a rocky bluff on the north-west ridge of Carn Ban. Above this the slopes steepen until they reach a gentle, broad ridge which follows the edge of vegetated cliffs overlooking Toll Lochan. The final rounded summit dome is featureless and boulder-strewn and carries a squat cairn.

An interesting return route descends the very steep grassy slopes of upper Coire Mor. A splendid cascade courses down a black cliff, while other dripping crags complete the cirque. Once in the corrie, which is dreadfully hag-ridden in places, follow the burn down to the loch.

Next page: The headwall of Coire Mor seen from the summit plateau of Seana Bhraigh. Photo: Tom Rix.

8 COIGACH

The name Coigach is given to the broad limb of land which is bounded by Loch Broom in the south and the Cam Loch–Loch Veyatie–Fionn Loch interlinked system in the north. It is characterised by a group of extraordinary individual mountains which burst into view as you drive north from Ullapool.

Basically, the landforms result from the shoreline of an ancient submerged continent, one of the first land masses in the world. The underlying platform is of grey, crumpled Lewisian gneiss, well over a thousand million years old, on which was deposited a layer of red Torridonian sandstone up to 7000 feet thick. Later, in Cambrian times, a layer of quartzite was laid over the sandstone and, in places such as the summit of Cul Mor, it still remains, the hard rock protecting the sandstone from erosion.

Millions of years of weathering and a succession of ice ages have worn down the sandstone, leaving just the relics which we see today: the complex ridges and corries of Ben Mor Coigach, the fortress of Cul Mor, the cones of Beinn an Eoin and Cul Beag and the perfect miniature of Stac Pollaidh.

The importance of Coigach has been recognised by the establishment of the Inverpolly Nature Reserve, the second largest in Scotland, which covers the area north of Loch Lurgainn and is administered by Scottish Natural Heritage. South of Loch Lurgainn, Ben Mor Coigach and its outliers make up a Grade I Site of Special Scientific Interest and form part of the Scottish Wildlife Trust's largest reserve.

Ben Mor Coigach from the A835 north of Ullapool. Photo: Ian Evans.

Ben Mor Coigach 2438ft/743m

Start/Finish: Culnacraig (064039) or
Finish: Old Drumrunie Lodge (166053)
Map: O.S. 1:50,000 Sheet 15
Distance: Culnacraig round, 6 miles/10km
　　　　　Complete traverse, 8 miles/13km
Time: Culnacraig round, 4–5 hours
　　　　Complete traverse, 5–6 hours
Grading: Both routes easy, although many variations are possible on the rocky south-western spur.

Just three miles north of Ullapool the great wall of Ben Mor Coigach, with its numerous buttresses and gullies, rises steeply above Ardmair Bay and provides a harsh backcloth to one of the classic views in the Western Highlands. Waves lap the parabolic curve of shingle, colourful boats bob at their moorings and, if you look out west on a fine evening as the sun is sinking, Isle Martin and a myriad Summer Islands can be seen floating on a mirror sea, set against a crimson sky.

The south-west ridge of Ben Mor Coigach rises abruptly from the sea and extends for a mile to the main summit on the eastern side of the massif. The complexity of the mountain is not obvious to the car driver, either on the main A835 or the narrow road to Achiltibuie, for behind the main ridge and the outlier of Beinn an Eoin lies an unspoilt wilderness of glens, corries, lochans and cliffs. This area, which has a rich and diverse flora and fauna, is a Grade I SSSI and is administered by the Scottish Wildlife Trust.

Next page: The Summer Isles in the mouth of Loch Broom seen here from the weathered sandstone ridge of Ben Mor Coigach. Photo: Richard Gilbert.

By far the most rewarding ascent of Ben Mor Coigach starts from the whitewashed cottages at Culnacraig, just beyond Achiltibuie. Cross the burn and make a rising traverse over rough ground to meet the Allt nan Coisiche just before it thunders down a ravine under the western prow of the main ridge (Garbh Choireachan).

A delightful scramble up the weathered sandstone brings you onto the ridge. You can pick your own way over the towers, savouring the coarse texture of the rock or following a network of sandy paths that wind up between the buttresses. The position is open and the view south across Loch Broom is peerless: directly below, the little prawners from Ullapool can be seen attending their creels, beyond Beinn Ghobhlach rises An Teallach, the massive peaks of Torridon and Flowerdale and the distant Cuillin of Skye. To the west you can see right across the Minch to the low outline of the Harris hills.

The ridge itself is quite narrow but for the timid walker, sheep paths contour under the pinnacles and gendarmes. After descend-

ing to a bealach the ridge merges with the main peak of Ben Mor Coigach and gentle boulder-strewn slopes lead up to the cairn and a massive windbreak.

If you can arrange for transport to meet you at Drumrunie, at the junction of the Achiltibuie road with the A835, it makes a satisfactory day to descend Ben Mor Coigach by the broad east ridge which runs over Beinn Tarsuinn. Easy but boggy moorland then leads to the road near the Allt Liathdoire bridge.

Alternatively, follow the north-facing cliffs round to Sgurr an Fhidhleir (the Fiddler), and marvel at this extraordinary blade of rock which rises sheer from Lochan Tuath to make Ben Mor Coigach's finest summit and best viewpoint. The ascent of the Fiddler's overlapping slabs is one of the most serious and committing rock climbs in the north-west.

Gentle slopes of deep heather and moorgrass now lead down the long Choire Reidh to Culnacraig.

Beinn an Eoin 2027ft/618m

Start/Finish: Loch Lurgainn (138066)
Map: O.S. 1:50,000 Sheet 15
Distance: 4 miles/6km
Time: 5 hours
Grading: Mainly easy but with a few steep, rocky slopes.

The twin summits of Beinn an Eoin, Sgorr Deas and Sgorr Tuath, are shapely cones of sandstone which rise high above the saturated moorland between Loch Lurgainn and the Ben Mor Coigach massif. Bare rock abounds on the summit ridges and broken crags fall away to the north and west giving stature to the hills which, because of their central position, provide the best possible views of the primeval Coigach landscape.

Beinn an Eoin is eminently suitable for a half-day excursion, perhaps after a morning's rain when the clouds clear from the west leaving the air washed and sparkling, or on a long summer evening. It is a modest walk which never fails to delight.

Park in a layby near the southern end of Loch Lurgainn and cross the inflowing burn on stepping stones. A path runs as far as the Feur-Loch but then you must make your own way towards

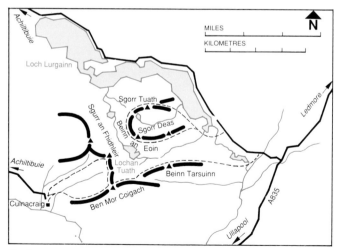

Previous page: Sgurr an Fhidhleir (Fiddler's Rock) of Ben Mor Coigach rises as a sheer blade of rock above Lochan Tuath. Photo: Iain Brown.

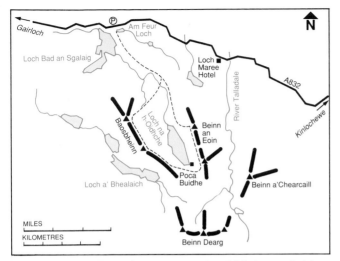

the abrupt spur of Cioch Beinn an Eoin which is guarded by a fringe of crags. Turn these on the south side and scramble up deep heather to gain the main ridge where you will find slabs of smooth sandstone.

Follow the broad ridge easily round to Sgorr Deas enjoying a dramatic view of the stupendous rock prow of Sgurr an Fhidhleir (the Fiddler), which thrusts out from the long north-west ridge of Ben Mor Coigach rising 300m sheer above Lochan Tuath.

Make a descending traverse to the delightful lochan under Sgorr Tuath where waders can often be seen strutting along the sandy shore. This is a sheltered spot for a break before tackling the rather loose rocky ridge to Sgorr Tuath, whose summit block is deeply split and fissured. (A serious hazard in thick mist or whiteout conditions.)

Proceeding east the ridge has been sculptured by the weather into weird pinnacles and towers, making an ideal foreground for views north to Stac Pollaidh, Suilven, Cul Mor and Quinag.

Easy, but rather boggy, slopes lead down southwards to a wide corrie. Cross this and contour under the Cioch to regain the car.

Cul Beag 2523ft/769m

Start/Finish: Linneraineach (126090)
Map: O.S. 1:50,000 Sheet 15
Distance: 6 miles/10km (4 miles/6km for direct way)
Time: 5–6 hours (3–4 hours)
Grading: Easy apart from a steep descent to the Coich a' Chuil Bhig bealach. (Direct way easy.)

In many ways Cul Beag is the mirror image of Sgorr Tuath, its neighbour across Loch Lurgainn. Both peaks have bold shapes, summits ringed by cliffs which rise from deep carpets of heather and bilberry and both are easily accessible from the Achiltibuie road.

The most direct and simple ascent of Cul Beag is from the roadside at the south end of Loch Lurgainn. Pick your way through the rocky bluffs and shallow gullies to gain the broad south shoulder which leads straight to the summit cairn perched on the edge of the cliffs. You can descend to the tiny lochan under Meall Dearg, climb to this subsidiary summit, contour round to the south shoulder and thus regain your route of ascent.

A much more worthwhile expedition is to proceed further along Loch Lurgainn, approaching the cottage of Linneraineach, and take the stalkers' path that starts by a small plantation and runs north to Loch an Doire Dhuibh.

Leaving the path at the south end of the loch, swing south-east to Lochan Dearg, to circumnavigate the line of cliffs on the north side of Cul Beag and Meall Dearg. When a line of weakness appears, scramble up the eastern slopes of Meall Dearg and thence gain the summit of Cul Beag. Throughout this ascent you are enjoying views of the fearsome precipices which guard the south side of Cul Mor.

Cul Beag may be descended directly to the bealach under Cioch a' Chuil Bhig, the prominent rocky satellite on the north side. From here the stalkers' path is regained near Loch Fhionnlaidh.

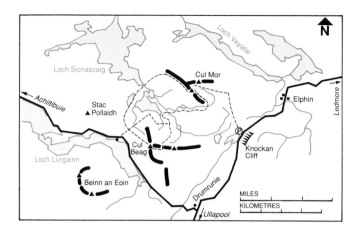

Stac Pollaidh 2011ft/613m

> Start/Finish: Inverpolly Nature Reserve car park (108095)
> Map: O.S. 1:50,000 Sheet 15
> Distance: 3 miles/5km
> Time: 3–4 hours
> Grading: Easy to the summit ridge. An exposed move up a rock step is needed to gain the true summit.

No walker who visits Coigach will be able to resist the ascent of Stac Pollaidh.

Stac Pollaidh, above all the peaks in Coigach, catches the eye because of its unique individuality and few peaks in Scotland make more of their modest height. As you drive north from Ullapool it bursts into view behind the tree-ringed loch at Drumrunie; dispensing with preliminaries it rises straight out of the moorland, thrusting jagged rack spires into the sky like a fossilised stegosaurus.

From the Nature Reserve car park beside Lock Lurgainn a path climbs three giant steps of ever increasing steepness straight to the summit ridge, while a newly constructed path swings round the east buttress and approaches the ridge from the north. The path is rather loose and bouldery at the top, but this should not deter you from making the ascent which will take about one hour and it is surprisingly strenuous.

As soon as you reach the summit ridge you are confronted by an astonishing panoramic view encompassing the indented western coastline, Cul Mor, Suilven, Canisp, Quinag and distant Foinaven. Find a sheltered nook amongst the rocks and enjoy one of the wildest scenes that Britain can offer. This is Norse

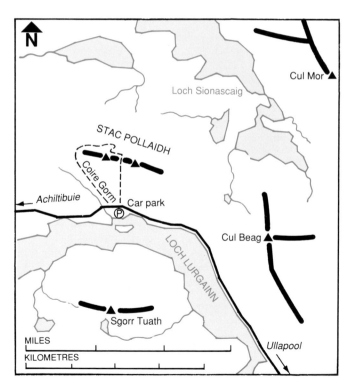

God country that never fails to thrill.

Experienced hill walkers can reach the highest (western) top of Stac Pollaidh by an exposed scramble along the very top of the sandstone ridge or via a path which winds in and out amongst an extraordinary array of turrets and pinnacles which have been sculptured by the weather over the ages.

An exposed move, the *mauvais-pas*, must be negotiated before you reach the western summit. This involves a 16ft/5m rock step on which there are excellent holds, but it needs a cool head, for a slip could have disastrous consequences. The inexperienced walker should leave this manoeuvre alone.

From the summit cairn return with care down the *mauvais-pas* and retrace your steps until you reach the top of a sandy scree run descending the northern slopes of Stac Pollaidh. A fast descent of the scree takes you to a traverse path which passes a tiny lochan under the towering west buttress and then leads you back, guided by cairns, to the car park.

Cul Mor 2786ft/849m

Start/Finish: Short route – Knockan (189094)
Long route – Linneraineach (126090)
Map: O.S. 1:50,000 Sheet 15
Distance: Short route, 7 miles/11km
Long route, 9 miles/14km
Time: Short route, 3–4 hours
Long route, 7 hours
Grading: Short route – Easy.
Long route – Steep scrambling up the nose of Cul Mor and careful route-finding needed on the descent.

Seen from the main A835 road Cul Mor tends to be dismissed as a shapeless hump although its twin peaks, connected by a curved ridge, gives it a crescent moon appearance when viewed from Elphin.

But Cul Mor well deserves its reputation as Coigach's most formidable peak. Not only does it stand head and shoulders above the other hills of Coigach but, on the north, south and west sides, great sweeps of bare rock rise to its summit plateau

and it has been likened to a fortress. In addition its impregnability from the south and west is enhanced by badly broken ground and an interlinked network of lochs and rivers which are unbridged.

By far the easiest and most popular route of ascent is from Knockan. Leave the car in a layby adjacent to a gate in the deer fence and take the well constructed stalkers' path which runs high onto the broad east shoulder of Cul Mor, marked Meallan Diomhain on the map.

Contour the wide corrie and the steep boulder field on the east side of Cul Mor to reach the small hanging corrie between the main peak and the subsidiary Creag nan Calman. This corrie leads easily to Cul Mor's rocky summit where sandstone gives way to a protective layer of quartzite. From the cairn you can gaze in wonderment across the watery wilderness to the Assynt hills of Suilven, Canisp and Quinag and west to the tiny islands of Enard Bay.

Walk round the sharp ridge of Creag nan Calman, where the small cairn is built on the edge of an abyss, and follow the ridge gently back down to the corrie.

A more exciting (but much more energetic and serious expedition) approaches Cul Mor from the west. Take the stalkers' path from Linneraineach to Lochan Gainmheich, passing a picturesque ruined stone cottage with rowan trees growing out of the doorway. The map clearly shows a bridge over the river linking the lochan with Loch Sionascaig, and ancient stone abutments can indeed be seen on each bank but the bridge is not there and the river must be forded. In normal conditions the river is not more than ankle deep but if the level is too high the expedition may be curtailed or aborted because a detour involves at least six extra rough miles.

The stubby western nose of Cul Mor rises ahead and a scrambling route can be found on the skyline ridge although care is needed in the loose gullies and over the chaotically piled blocks of sandstone. The position is airy and exhilarating, with an ever-widening view of the magnificent country of Coigach and Assynt gradually unfolding.

A broad ridge links the western nose with Cul Mor's main

summit whence you should head south to Creag nan Calman. Continue due east until you meet a burn and follow it as it rushes through a ravine on its way to Lochan Dearg a' Chuil Mhoir. This is a beautiful, lonely, shallow loch with sandy shores overhung by sheer cliffs. Keep to the left bank of the exit stream as it plunges down to Loch an Doire Dhuibh where you pick up the stalkers' path back to Linneraineach.

Sgorr Deas and Sgorr Tuath, the twin summits of Beinn an Eoin, make a pleasant half-day expedition. Photo: Jim Teesdale.

Below: *The unique Coigach scenery with Cul Mor (left) and Cul Beag (right) viewed from the summit rocks of Stac Pollaidh. Photo: Alan O'Brien.*

9 ASSYNT

In the previous chapter I described the view north from the saw-toothed summit ridge of Stac Pollaidh as looking over one of the wildest regions in Britain. This region is Assynt which extends from the west coast to Conival in the east and from the Loch Veyatie-Kirkaig river system in the south to Loch a'Chairn Bhain in the north.

Where else could you find mountains with the individuality of Suilven, Canisp and Quinag, remote bays studded with foam-flecked islands, sandy coves, towering cliffs, waterfalls, clear blue lochs, salmon rivers, woods of birch and rowan and a complex mixture of rocks (ancient Lewisian gneiss, Torridonian sandstone and Cambrian limestone) which have delighted generations of geologists?

The lonely lochs of Assynt are the home of a great many varieties of duck, as well as whooper swans and the delightful red-throated and black-throated divers.

Few roads run through Assynt: the main road north to Kylesku and its branch to Lochinver, and a single track road (with passing places) that winds round the bays and inlets of the coast, passing through Inverkirkaig, Lochinver, Stoer and Drumbeg. Lochinver is by far the largest village in Assynt and it is an important white fish port which has recently been extensively modernised with a grant from the EEC.

Several holidays would be necessary to explore adequately all the hills, glens, rivers, lochs and bays of Assynt but the list of walks that I describe below will give you a taste of its principal delights. If time restricts you to just one mountain from the list, make it Suilven.

The distinctive silhouette of Suilven, which dominates the Assynt region in spite of its modest height, is seen here from Elphin. Photo: Phil Cooper.

Round of the Cam Loch

> *Start/Finish: Elphin (214119)*
> *Map: O.S. 1:50,000 Sheet 15*
> *Distance: 8 miles/13km*
> *Time: 4 hours*
> *Grading: A delightful walk around one of Assynt's most beautiful lochs. Much of the walk is trackless.*

The Cam Loch is one of many deep, clear lakes in the Coigach/Assynt area. Winter storms drive angry white horses across the surface to break on the shingly shore and I have seen curtains of spray racing down the loch like dervishes. Yet in high summer the sun shimmers and sparkles on the bluest of water, waders turn over the stones and, in places, birch and rowan grow on low cliffs above the shore.

A circuit of the Cam Loch takes you into the heart of the wildest country of Assynt and provides intimate views of Cul Mor and Suilven in particular.

From Elphin take the track to the fish hatchery beside the Abhainn Mor which links the Cam Loch and Loch Veyatie. The river is bridged near a waterfall and you should cross to the northern shore.

Head north-west, keeping to the high ground above the loch. You walk over rocky knobs and above decayed woodlands; there is no path and the going is rough.

As the Cam Loch narrows at its western end contour Creagan Mor and then pass over a line of crags to the inflowing stream. The stream is deep and wide. Don't attempt to cross it here but walk westwards until the level drops to ankle deep or less. This

is usually less than one kilometre from the loch.

The walk back to Elphin along the northern shore of the Cam Loch is most enjoyable. You can choose to keep to the rough moorland above the loch or walk over the pebbles on the shore itself where there is much of interest.

Half-way along the loch you meet the stalkers' path which runs west to Loch na Gainimh and which is used for the first part of the Suilven east-west traverse. This path proves a bonus for tired legs.

Suilven 2399ft/731m: The East-West Traverse

> *Start: Elphin (230121)*
> *Finish: Lochinver (093223)*
> *Map: O.S. 1:50,000 Sheet 15*
> *Distance: 16 miles/26km*
> *Time: 9–10 hours*
> *Grading: A stiff walk over remote and rough country. Some exposed scrambling on Suilven's east ridge.*

Driving north from Ullapool the visitor to Wester Ross and Sutherland is constantly stimulated by the mountains of Coigach: the great wedge of Cul Beag, the perfect cockscomb of Stac Pollaidh and the thrusting blade of the Fiddler. But just beyond Cul Mor's twin peaks, as you descend gently to the crofting community of Elphin, Suilven bursts into view. At first you rub your eyes with disbelief at this monster whale-back rising isolated and inexorably steeply from a flattish base of Lewisian gneiss. Suilven's sublime shape grows on you over the years like a great work of art. It sets the nerves tingling and it nourishes the soul.

Suilven, like many of its neighbours in Coigach and Assynt, is a sandstone peak whose rock was laid down in warm seas in the late pre-Cambrian era and the parallel strata can clearly be seen picked out by the rays of the evening sun.

Unless you are prepared to swim, a direct approach from the south is impossible because Suilven is guarded by Loch Veyatie and the Fionn Loch which interlink to form a ten mile long stretch

From the Kirkaig River approach on the south side Suilven bursts into view across Fionn Loch. Photo: Tom Rix.

of water. Again, a direct ascent of the western prow, Caisteal Liath (the Grey Castle), necessitates rock climbing and, rearing above the fishing village of Lochinver, it looks most intimidating.

This leaves us with ascents of the two loose, steep gullies which run down north and south from the lowest point of the ridge, Bealach Mor, or a scramble up the eastern summit of Meall Beag.

The eastern approach is by far the most rewarding, for it involves a long walk across typically rough Sutherland moorland, some airy scrambling to reach Suilven's crest and the negotiation of an exposed *mauvais-pas*.

Walkers who are nervous of steep rock or suffer from vertigo should restrict their routes to the Bealach Mor gullies, for Suilven is a serious mountain which takes no prisoners. There are no escape routes and help is far away. In spring when the gullies are packed with hard icy snow it is essential to use ice axe and crampons.

Just north of Elphin the road crosses the Ledmore River by a stone bridge. You can leave the car 50m beyond the bridge in a layby which also marks the start of a stalkers' path running along the north shore of the Cam Loch.

Early on a spring morning the Cam Loch is peerless. Small waders strut along the stony shore, gorse buds open in the sunshine, rowan and birch trees hang over the water from rocky bluffs and primroses peep shyly from sheltered nooks. On my last visit there was not a breath of wind and Cul Mor was mirrored with astonishing clarity in the still water, kestrels played 'catch-me-if-you-can' above us and a skein of honking geese flew past high in the sky.

As so often happens the path is excellent to begin with but soon deteriorates and becomes boggy and less distinct. After crossing the Loch a 'Chroisg burn it leaves the Cam Loch and climbs north up the hillside, a few cairns helping you locate its route through the heather and tussocks.

All this time the superb eastern abutment of Suilven attracts the eye. It looks desperately distant but infinitely desirable and motivation is no problem. At this stage leave the path and strike boldly uphill making for the broad shoulder of Meall na Braclaich. This brings you out of very thick and tangled heather onto slabs of smooth sandstone and erratics. Striding out confidently

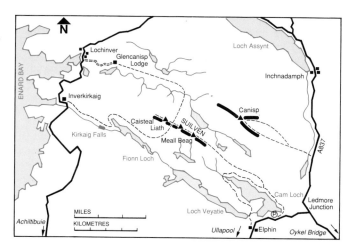

Firstly you must step across a deep fissure in the sandstone strata, where the ridge narrows dramatically, and then you arrive above a sheer 100ft cliff with no apparent point of weakness. This, the *mauvais pas*, can be turned by descending rather steep rocks on the north side to gain a weak traverse line running west to the dark, dank bealach which is overhung by dripping crags. It is a relief to climb steeply up to Meall Mheadhonach by a loose zig-zag path.

Another scrambly descent is necessary to reach the broad grassy slopes running down to Bealach Mor. An old wall, still in remarkably good repair, runs across the ridge at this point and you can peer down the gully on the north side, your eventual route of descent from Suilven.

One perfect spring day I cut steps up the frozen snow packing this gully to emerge into warm, bright sunshine, where I surprised a pair of gleaming black ravens courageously mobbing a golden eagle that had entered their territory.

On now easily to the turf covered dome of Caisteal Liath, (2399ft/731m) which looks over Lochinver, Ennard Bay and north to the island dotted bay of Eddrachillis, a perfect example of the close affinity of mountains, wild coastline and seascape which characterises North West Scotland.

It is all too easy to dream the afternoon away on this most exquisite of Scottish peaks, but the toy-like boats in Lochinver harbour and the distant white line of breakers on the rocky shore bring home to you the task ahead. So it is back down to Bealach Mor and the unpleasantly loose gully which eventually leads to easy, if boggy, ground above the west end of Loch na Gainimh.

On lower ground you meet a well constructed stalkers' path which crosses the Abhainn na Craich Airigh by a wooden bridge and continues easily down the glen. At the ruined crofting settlement of Suileag another path runs north to meet the A837 at Little Assynt House but you should continue westwards over a few minor hillocks to Glencanisp Lodge.

This beautiful stone house in the best Scottish tradition looks over the reedy Loch Druim Suardalain. In spring the approach path is bright with gorse, primroses, violets and buttercups and

now you can appreciate the magnificent scenery: both Canisp to the north and Cul Mor to the south considerably overlook Suilven but their symmetry is no match for the latter's dramatic form.

You look down on watery wastes: the Cam Loch, Loch Veyatie and Loch Sionascaig with its tree covered islands while smaller, shallower lochans fill every hollow.

Seen head-on during the long approach from Elphin, Suilven's east ridge has appeared daunting but, as you get closer, the angle seems to ease and your confidence grows. In fact you can scramble up almost anywhere; the spur is ledgy and well supplied with good hand-holds and it provides a truly exhilarating climb.

Pause awhile on the rounded summit of Meall Beag and enjoy the panoramic views extending from Foinaven, Arkle and Quinag to Ben More Assynt, Conival and Seana Bhraigh and due south to Stac Pollaidh and the Coigach hills. The view west along the ridge is effectively blocked by massive Meall Mheadhonach, Suilven's second highest summit, which is not particularly easily climbed from any direction.

the woods resound to birdsong, while hundreds of daffodils surround the lawns. The right-of-way runs behind the house through luxuriant rhododendrons to meet the private road to Lochinver.

The walk ends as splendidly as it began, for you suddenly round a corner to be confronted by the busy harbour of Lochinver with its brightly painted cottages and fishing boats. On one arm of the bay stands the stone-built Culag Hotel which looks rather gaunt and cold but can be guaranteed to meet your immediate requirements.

Suilven: the North-South Traverse

Start: Lochinver (093223)
Finish: Inverkirkaig (085193)
Map: O.S. 1:50,000 Sheet 15
Distance: 15 miles/24km
Time: 8–9 hours
Grading: A long day in remote, mountainous country. Two steep and rather loose gullies must be negotiated on Suilven itself.

The north-south traverse of Suilven is a long but less daunting expedition than the east-west traverse described above, for the route avoids the *mauvais pas* on Meall Beag and it follows a path the whole way.

From Lochinver take the road to Glencanisp Lodge and the continuation stalkers' path past Suileag to just short of Loch na Gainimh. A cairn marks the turn off to Suilven and a very boggy path runs up the hillside to the gully descending north from Bealach Mor. Scramble up this loose and tedious gully to reach the bealach and thence the summit of Suilven.

Return to the bealach and descend scree slopes in the wider south-facing gully to meet a narrow path along the north bank of the Fionn Loch. This eventually rounds the western end of the loch to join the tourist trail beside the Kirkaig river.

Make the short (signed) diversion to see the Kirkaig Falls. This impressive waterfall plunges into a deep, dark pool set romantically amidst crags and trees and it forms an impasse for salmon. In season they can be seen leaping and flashing through rainbow spray in a vain attempt to proceed up river.

Two more miles of pleasant walking take you to the car park at Inverkirkaig bridge, where you should arrange to meet your transport. Alternatively continue another three miles (5km) along the road into Lochinver.

Canisp 2776ft/846m

Start/Finish: On the A837 north of Loch Awe (252166)
Map: O.S. 1:50,000 Sheet 15
Distance: 9 miles/14km
Time: 5 hours
Grading: Easy.

I have great affection for Canisp. It sits like a slice of cheese on the waterlogged moorland north of Suilven and, having no dramatic features, it is an unassuming mountain. It is also a very easy mountain and its long and gentle eastern slopes are suitable for a leisurely family outing, yet its height puts both haughty Suilven and Quinag to shame and provides perhaps the best viewpoint of all.

The approach to Canisp from the A837 road just north of Loch Awe is rough and boggy, but the higher you climb the more rocky the mountain becomes and the firmer the ground underfoot.

Make for the broad south-east ridge which encloses the shallow upper corrie of Canisp and hug the edge to enjoy the magnificent view south to Suilven. You climb over some quartzite outcrops before reaching the rocky summit plateau and a substantial man-made windbreak enclosing the cairn.

On the north side you look over a steep escarpment to Loch Assynt, Quinag and the hills of the Reay Forest. A broad ridge runs down in a north-westerly direction to a saddle, whence an easy descent can be made to the south end of Loch Gainimh. Strong walkers who can arrange transport at Lochinver may wish to return to the fishing port along the good stalkers' path running north of the loch to Glencanisp Lodge which is described in the Suilven section.

You can return to the road via the boulder field on the north side of Canisp's upper corrie and the shoulder of Meall Diamhain. In hot weather several of the clear, secluded lochans west of Loch Awe are ideal for an impromptu swim.

Breabag 2674ft/815m

Start: Lyne, near Ledmore Junction (249141)
Finish: Inchnadamph (252217)
Map: O.S. 1:50,000 Sheet 15
Distance: 9 miles/14km
Time: 6–7 hours
Grading: Easy, if rough, walking over a remote and rarely visited summit which is a spectacular viewpoint.

Conival, whose steep summit slopes of grey quartzite make it such a spectacular mountain rising inland from Inchnadamph at the head of Gleann Dubh, is really the centre point of a long and broad ridge running all the way from Glas Bheinn in the north to Breabag in the south.

The ridge extending to Glas Bheinn has been described in glowing terms elsewhere in this book but Breabag, which in many respects reflects its northern counterpart, makes an equally special, if somewhat shorter, expedition. If Quinag is the dominant neighbour of Glas Bheinn then Ben More Assynt, seen towering above Dubh Loch Mor, provides the backcloth to Breabag.

To avoid a tiresome five mile walk back to the starting point near Ledmore Junction, transport should be arranged at Inchnadamph, although it is usually very easy to obtain a lift on the A837.

Start from the bridge over the Ledbeg river near the mound of stones labelled *Chambered Cairn* on the map. Walk up the track to the locked and empty cottage at Lyne. Here the path ceases and you must make your own way through the bracken, heather and rough grass heading up towards Creag Liath. A streak of light coloured scree makes Creag Liath very conspicuous from afar, but you should aim well south of the main scree slopes.

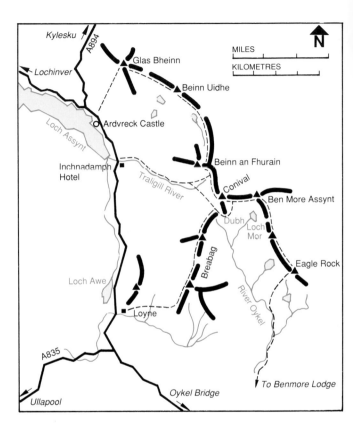

This side of the mountain is popular with deer and I passed several herds which paused for a moment, watching me with heads erect, before melting away up the hillside.

Tongues of quartzite boulders run down through the heather but it is relatively easy to find a way onto the upper plateau without too much scree bashing. Streams of ice cold water emerge at the perimeter of the boulder fields and the ground is bright with thyme and clumps of sea pinks. The hillside far below is scarred by a working marble quarry.

The summit of Breabag carries a small cairn and a windbreak where the best views are northwards to the superb corrie between Conival and Ben More Assynt, which holds a green lochan sparkling beneath the cliffs and sheets of grey quartzite screes. The long ridge running south-east from Ben More Assynt to Carn nan Conbhairean is particularly prominent, while to the west Canisp and Suilven steal the show.

As you progress north the broad ridge becomes knobbly and rocky with lochans filling every scoop and hollow in the shelving quartzite. Three east-facing corries, Coirean Ban and Glas Choire Mor and Beag, lie below the ridge. They are exceptionally fine and wild and it is well worth hugging the eastern edge to peer into them as you walk to Point 715m.

From Breabag Tarsuinn, broken slopes can be descended to the bealach under Conival, whence the path down into Gleann Dubh is far from distinct for a while; it is best to keep well to the north of the burn which runs through a succession of ravines. A good path is reached either at the upper caves or further north at the trade route from the Conival-Beinn an Fhurain bealach.

Conival 3238ft/987m and Ben More Assynt 3274ft/998m

Start/Finish: Inchnadamph (252217)
Map: O.S. 1:50,000 Sheet 15
Distance: 11 miles/18km
Time: 7 hours
Grading: A rough and remote mountain walk involving steep slopes of sharp quartzite boulders and an exposed rocky ridge.

The main A837 road through Assynt divides the prominent, individual, sandstone peaks on the west side (Canisp, Suilven, Cul Mor) from a long line of interconnected quartzite peaks on the east. This huge massif rises considerably higher than the more westerly peaks and boasts two Munros (Ben More Assynt and Conival) and two Corbetts (Breabag and Glas Bheinn).

Although these hills can be climbed from upper Glen Oykel, the approach march is extremely long and Inchnadamph makes the most convenient base.

Inchnadamph is a small settlement in an area of Durness limestone; the resulting increase in soil pH gives lush grasslands, rich flora and excellent grazing. Much of this area is a National Nature Reserve. The large whitewashed hotel is popular with walkers, fishermen, geologists and naturalists.

Conival stands aloof at the head of Gleann Dubh, distinguished by horizontal strata running across the bare quartzite face of its upper tier. Ben More Assynt lies out of sight one mile east of Conival and the two hills are usually climbed together.

Take the Land Rover track which runs up beside the Traligill river to just beyond the cottage of Glenbain. In one place the river emerges from under a limestone cliff and, further up the glen, a number of caves can be seen. If time allows you can bring a torch and amuse yourself exploring some of these underground chambers.

From Gleann Dubh it looks tempting to make straight for Conival's summit, but a ring of crags guards this direct approach. Keep to the rather muddy path beside the river which leads you into a shallow, bouldery corrie under the broad bealach between the northernmost subsidiary summit of Conival and the 2821ft/860m top of Beinn an Fhurain. Rough stony slopes now lead easily to the summit of Conival where some rock outcrops make a useful windbreak.

A rather steep and scrambly descent of Conival's eastern spur takes you to a low bealach and the start of the long west ridge of Ben More Assynt. The going is easy but rough over the blocks of angular quartzite; it is also quite airy in places and you enjoy wonderful views north to the rocky, watery landscape of upper Glen Coul and the distant hills of the Reay Forest.

Ben More Assynt sports several rock castles, each with its own cairn. Take your pick but don't dawdle for it is a long road home.

The quickest way back to Inchnadamph is to retrace your steps over Conival and regain Gleann Dubh by your route of

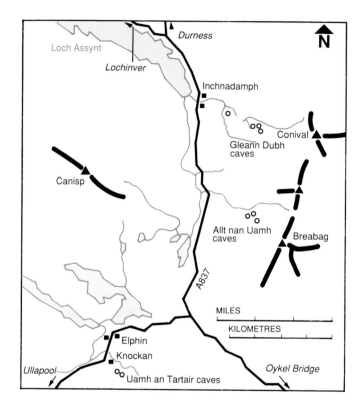

south from the summit of Ben More Assynt to Carn nan Conbhairean and thence into Glen Oykel, reaching the road via Benmore Lodge.

Leaving Ben More Assynt the ridge is narrow with one or two tight squeezes around gendarmes which threaten to throw you off balance down the slopes. It should not be underestimated in winter conditions when ice axe and crampons may be needed. At Carn nan Conbhairean, though, the ridge widens and becomes more gentle in its descent.

Below, to the south, lies Dubh Loch Mor, a perfect corrie lochan surrounded by a cirque of vegetated and deeply seamed cliffs. This scenery, together with the exceptionally wild and rocky country spreading away northwards, makes this (longer) descent route from Ben More Assynt an airy and exhilarating experience.

If energy can be dredged up from the reserves it is worthwhile making the easy ascent of Eagle Rock and then descending to the ather indistinct and boggy path that runs down to Benmore Lodge beside Loch Ailsh. A three mile private motor road links the Lodge with the A837; it is pleasant to stroll beside the loch watching the birdlife but the last stretch is spoilt by newly planted forestry.

Glas Bheinn 2546ft/776m from Inchnadamph

Start/Finish: Inchnadamph (252217)
Map: O.S. 1:50,000 Sheet 15
Distance: 13 miles/21km
Time: 7–8 hours
Grading: A most rewarding walk over rough and rarely visited hills.

The well beaten track up Gleann Dubh, from Inchnadamph to the bealach under the north ridge of Conival, is used principally by walkers set on collecting the Munros of Conival and Ben More Assynt. Very few head north along the broad ridge

Ardvreck Castle and the Spidean Coinich summit of Quinag seen across Loch Assynt. Photo: Stephen Greenwood.

ascent. But a pleasant alternative is to return to the bealach east of Conival and descend the grand Garbh Choire until it is possible to work your way westwards, underneath cliffs, to reach the Conival-Breabag Tarsuinn bealach. Follow the Allt a'Bhealaich down into Gleann Dubh, meeting the path near the caves just two miles from Inchnadamph.

A third choice for the super-fit party that can arrange transport on the Bonar Bridge road (296083) is to descend the ridge

running for six miles over Beinn an Fhurain and Beinn Uidhe to the distant Corbett of Glas Bheinn. Yet this ridge gives an unforgettable walk over wild and trackless mountains with open and extensive views across Sutherland. It is a walk for the connoisseur.

Take the path to the bealach, described in the Conival-Ben More Assynt chapter, and climb the boulder-strewn slopes to reach the top of the sheer rock buttresses on Na Tuadhan (Pt 860m). Pause awhile and enjoy the croaking of ravens and a wide view to Beinn Leoid, Meallan Liath Coire Mhic Dhughaill, Ben Hope and the islands of Eddrachillis Bay.

Follow the edge of the considerable north-facing quartzite cliffs for another mile before heading off for Loch nan Cuaran. The going underfoot is incredibly tough with extensive sheets of shattered quartzite, wrinkled and split by 10,000 winters since the glaciers retreated. In summer you can enjoy watching families of young ptarmigan amongst the rocks and smelling the sun-warmed thyme and clumps of scabious. Deep lochans of crystal clear water fill the many scoops and hollows.

After crossing the wide plateau of Beinn Uidhe and descending to a bealach, you meet an unexpectedly sharp little ridge up to the summit of Glas Bheinn which gives a unique view into the deep corries of Quinag.

Easy but stony slopes lead down in a south-westerly direction to lower ground near Achmore Farm. Here a Land Rover track leads to the main road near Ardvreck Castle, less than two miles from Inchnadamph.

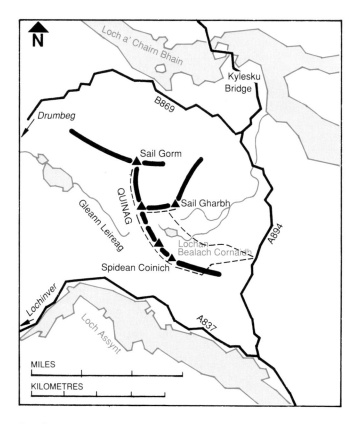

Quinag 2651ft/808m

Start/Finish: Summit of A894 north of Skiag Bridge (232273)
Map: O.S. 1:50,000 Sheet 15
Distance: 8 miles/13km
Time: 6 hours
Grading: A fine mountain walk with many superb positions. It should present no difficulties in good conditions.

Assynt provides many classic mountain views: Suilven from Elphin or Lochinver, the white quartzite bulk of Conival rising above the Traligill river at Inchnadamph and the Stack of Glencoul from Kylesku. But my favourite is that of the rock turret of Quinag's Spidean Coinich set against a blue sky on a breezy summer's day when the white horses on Loch Assynt break on the shore beside the romantic sixteenth century ruin of Ardvreck Castle.

Quinag looks regal from every direction. Unrelentingly steep slopes, weathered in places into sheer cliffs, fall from the Y-shaped ridges which enclose deep corries. There is little level ground and the switchback nature of Quinag's main spine has won it the status of three distinct Corbetts.

There is much steep, rocky ground on Quinag and in conditions of mist, high wind or snow and ice it should only be attempted by experienced and well-equipped parties. But in summer the high ridges give exhilarating walking with stirring views over the western seaboard.

It is a bonus to start this walk from near the high point on the Skiag Bridge to Kylesku road at about 250m. Leave the car in an old quarry on the east side of the road and cross a short and boggy stretch of moorland to gain the east ridge of Spidean Coinich. You soon reach scoured slabs of quartzite which later give way to fissured sandstone leading up to a subsidiary summit under Spidean Coinich. Now keep to the right (north) side of the ridge, just above an impressive line of cliffs which provide a taste of exposure.

From Spidean Coinich descend a steep and narrow rock ridge which runs north to a lesser summit before dropping again to Bealach a'Cornaidh. Look back at the towering sandstone buttresses falling from the summit of Spidean Coinich towards the corrie lochan.

Scramble up to Point 745m, descend to a bealach on the north side, climb over a flat topped castle of rock and then walk along a windswept, boulder-strewn ridge to Sail Gorm at 2546ft/776m. Several crazy pinnacles and razor sharp spurs are passed on the west side of the ridge.

Enjoy the view over Eddrachillis Bay before retracing your steps to Point 745m. It is worth making the short detour across a grassy saddle to gain Quinag's true summit, the trig pillar at 2651ft/808m on Sail Gharbh.

Return to the saddle and scramble down loose south-facing slopes towards Lochan Bealach Cornaidh. Surprisingly a stalkers' path appears through the rough tussocky grass, boulders and heather, and leads you rapidly back to the road.

The Stack of Glencoul 1621ft/494m

Start/Finish: Unapool (238328)
Map: O.S. 1:50,000 Sheet 15
Distance: 18 miles/29km
Time: 9–10 hours
Grading: A long expedition through uninhabited, barren and rugged mountain country.

The mighty north face of Quinag's Sail Gharbh towers over the new Kylesku bridge, every seam highlighted by the slanting rays of evening sunshine. Yet the view east down Loch Glencoul is equally impressive. Here is a region of bare rock faces, deep gorges and chunky peaks of ancient Lewisian gneiss. Particularly prominent is the grey turrett, the Stack of Glencoul, which rears over Loch Beag at the head of Loch Glencoul.

The ascent of the Stack requires fitness and commitment but connoisseurs of wild hill country will find ample reward.

From the hamlet of Unapool, near Kylesku, you must tackle the trackless, tussocky and boggy ground on the south shore of Loch Glencoul. But in summer you can delight in the seals sunning themselves on the rocks, and the dragonflies, foxgloves, cottongrass, bog asphodel, buttercups and bog myrtle.

Near the headland overlooking Eilean an Tuim, a cliff must be traversed by a narrow and exposed path that twists and turns across its steep face above the loch.

This section needs great care: a geology student from Leeds University fell and was seriously injured here. As a result of this accident, guidelines were laid down concerning the supervision of parties in the hills.

South of Loch Beag, ford the river and weave your way up through rocky outcrops to the Stack of Glencoul. Here, in a cool, shady gully bright with yellow saxifrage, I once disturbed a ring ouzel.

The glen of the Abhainn an Loch Bhig is an exceptionally steep, rocky defile and, on the south side, the famous waterfall, Eas a'Chual Aluinn, roars down from the lip in a streak of foam for 650ft. Extraordinarily, this fall is complemented by another cascade of white water falling from a similar height on the north side.

The Stack (1621ft/494m) is the blunt end of a ridge, holding many lochans, which divides the massifs of Beinn Leoid and Ben More Assynt.

Scramble down between cliffs to Glen Coul, walk under some enormous bare rock walls to Glencoul House, and cross the rough hillside to Loch Glendhu. The head of Gleann Dubh is another fascinating area of woods and crags.

Cross the river by a footpath and begin the long walk back to Unapool. This is a lovely, peaceful walk at the end of such a rugged day; the path runs above the loch where the water is so clear you can see down to the rocks on the sea-bed, entwined with fronds of seaweed and dotted with sea urchins. You cross the sizeable Maldie Burn below a splendid waterfall and meet the main road again at Kylestrome. Return to Unapool over the smart new Kylesku bridge.

Beinn Leoid 2598ft/792m

Start/Finish: Kylesku (230338)
Map: O.S. 1:50,000 Sheet 15
Distance: 9 miles round trip from Loch Beag
Time: 5–6 hours
Grading: An excellent stalkers' path gives access to this rough peak. Availability of boats may demand a tight schedule.

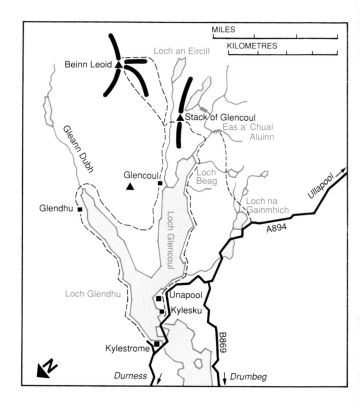

If you have enjoyed the ascent of the Stack of Glencoul you will be keen to return to this wild and seldom visited area of Sutherland. The Corbett of Beinn Leoid makes a thoroughly worthwhile objective but, be warned, it is a remote mountain requiring stamina and determination.

One way of approaching Beinn Leoid is from Glen Coul, which itself can be reached via the narrow coast path from Unapool which runs beside Loch Glencoul and is described in the ascent of the Stack of Glencoul. But a completely different method of approach, and one that I was fortunate in being able to use, is to go by boat from Kylesku to Loch Beag. In the

summer regular boat trips operate from Kylesku, running down Loch Glencoul into Loch Beag for holidaymakers to see the seals and marvel at the Eas a'Chual Aluinn waterfall. A co-operative skipper will drop you off from the morning trip and collect you again later in the day. My particular arrangements gave me five hours ashore which is just enough to climb Beinn Leoid and return, but leaves no time for dawdling. A more generous schedule would be preferable. If you miss the boat be prepared for an extra two hour's walk back to Unapool.

From the locked cottage of Glencoul a fine path runs up the glen. The path has recently been re-paved with boulders to facilitate access for deer stalking and for anglers bound for the high Loch an Eireill, where an upturned boat can be seen above the shore at the northern end.

The path climbs steeply up Glen Coul. On the north side it is overlooked by a fearsome line of crags while the Stack of Glencoul rears above to the south. Where the glen levels out, a magnificent waterfall spills over a black cliff. Together with Eas a'Chual Aluinn and its mirror image across the glen this makes three superlative falls all within a tiny area of this astonishing wilderness which abounds in bare rock.

The line of cliffs on the north side gradually peters out and when Loch Eireill is reached tongues of grass run down to the water's edge. This is as good a place as any to commence the climb to Beinn Leoid.

The going is easy, though rather hag ridden, and the slopes rise relentlessly until the final cone of Beinn Leoid is reached. This consists of lichen covered boulder scree which is treacherously slippery when wet, but you soon arrive at the stone built trig pillar within a circular wind shelter.

Beinn Leoid is typical of many remote Corbetts in providing spectacular views from unusual angles of the surrounding hills. In this case you will enjoy the tremendously wild and rocky landscape north of Ben More Assynt, the Reay Forest, down Loch a'Chairn Bhain to the islands of Eddrachillis Bay and the incomparable indented coastline of Sutherland.

If you have a boat to catch you should return the same way but if you plan to walk out, follow the long north-west ridge leading to Gleann Dubh. Here you meet the excellent track running westwards alongside Loch Glendhu to Kylestrome, as described in the return route from the Stack of Glencoul.

The narrow road north of Lochinver provides spectacular views across Assynt to Canisp and Suilven. Photo: Alan O'Brien.

10 THE REAY FOREST

Under the great northern buttresses of Quinag lies Kylesku, now merely a hotel and a small collection of cottages perched above the shore of Loch a'Chairn Bhain. But, until a smart new curved concrete bridge opened in 1984, Kylesku was an important landmark on the road north where you queued for the car ferry across the loch to Kylestrome. This provided an opportunity to stretch your legs, fill your lungs with sea air and watch herons, shags and seals on the seaweed-covered skerries.

Beyond Kylesku we leave Assynt for another, even lonelier, wilderness area: the Reay Forest, once the hunting ground of the Lords of Reay who were chiefs of the Mackay clan, until one of the chiefs sold the land to the Duke of Sutherland in 1829.

The hills of the Reay Forest are mainly flat topped and, after the aberration of the Moine Thrust on Ben More Assynt, the correct geological order of rocks is restored with quartzite rising above a bedrock of Lewisian gneiss. A myriad hill lochs drain into the swift salmon rivers of Laxford, Rhiconich and Dionard.

Two superb mountains, Foinaven and Arkle, dominate the Reay Forest towering high above the scarred bedrock and haughtily commanding extensive views over much of Sutherland. It is little wonder that the Duchess of Westminster christened two brilliant thoroughbred racehorses after these majestic peaks.

Few walkers venture into the Reay Forest and beautiful, convoluted hills such as Meallan Liath Coire Mhic Dhughaill and the north side of Foinaven can be enjoyed in utter solitude.

In good weather conditions, which are a rare bonus in this area, five star days can be guaranteed in this undiscovered corner of the Highlands.

Looking north along the quartzite ridges of Foinaven. The principal summit, Ganu Mor, is on the right. Photo: Stephen Greenwood.

Ben Stack 2365ft/721m

Start/Finish: On the A838 near Lochstack Lodge (265437)
Map: O.S. 1:50,000 Sheet 9
Distance: 6 miles/10km
Time: 4–5 hours
Grading: An easy and varied walk over the most shapely peak in the Reay Forest.

In spite of its modest height Ben Stack is the most shapely of the Reay Forest peaks. It rises boldly above Loch Stack in a perfect cone, its sharp summit emphasised by a band of broken cliffs falling away on three sides.

Ben Stack is a rewarding peak to climb, for its summit rocks provide a mild scramble and it gives fine views north to Arkle and south to Assynt. For these reasons it is a popular objective for students from John Ridgeway's Adventure School at nearby Ardmore.

From Laxford Bridge drive south and park near a low stone cottage on the roadside opposite Lochstack Lodge. Take the wide stalkers' path that winds up the hillside towards Loch na Seilge. Above the loch a line of fence posts and a small cairn mark the turning off point for the west ridge of Ben Stack.

This broad and rather soggy ridge leads up, ever steepening, to the rock band where you can choose a variety of routes to the twin summits of Ben Stack.

A less steep descent down the grassy eastern shoulder takes you over a subsidiary summit to lower ground, and you can

Next page: Banded quartzite screes characterise the western slopes of Arkle, seen here across Loch Stack. Photo: Lucy Gilbert.

follow a path to the road beside Loch Stack. Don't try to cut corners by heading north too soon, or you will arrive at the edge of a long line of fearsome cliffs.

A very pleasant two mile stroll alongside the loch brings you back to your starting point.

Arkle 2582ft/787m

Start/Finish: Achfary (296402)
Map: O.S. 1:50,000 Sheet 9
Distance: 14 miles/22km
Time: 7–8 hours
Grading: A high mountain walk with some rough scrambling but a less serious expedition than Foinaven.

Leaving Scourie, the Durness road climbs to a high plateau overlooking the Reay Forest. From here the view north is dominated by the slumbering giant of Arkle, characterised by banded quartzite screes which gleam in the late afternoon sunshine or after rain.

But the rounded shoulders of Arkle enclose a huge and rugged north-facing corrie containing lonely Loch an Easain Uaine, while the full glory of Foinaven's main ridge rises beyond.

Several well-constructed stalkers' paths can be used conveniently to facilitate access to Arkle, both on the approach and return. Walkers who have struggled across the saturated moorland from Gualin House to the Ceann Garbh summit of Foinaven will be doubly appreciative.

Park at Achfary, between Lochs Stack and More, and walk along the rough road to the bothy of Lone. A good path continues on the north side of the Allt Horn which should be followed for a mile before striking up steep and even more bouldery slopes to the east ridge of Arkle.

Beyond the 2484ft/757m south summit of Arkle, which is marked by a large stone heap, the ridge narrows dramatically, in

Previous page: The extraordinary A'Cheir Ghorm ridge of Foinaven which makes an exciting route of ascent from Strath Dionard. Photo: Tom Rix.

one place to a wafer-thin edge. Some of the massive stone blocks across which you walk are split down the centre, leaving deep fissures resembling grykes in Yorkshire limestone pavements. Just before the main top, at 2582ft/787m, the boulders give way to a deep carpet of moss and the fat and well-built cairn is unmistakable.

The summit ridge now bends round to the north-east but after another half mile you should leave it and make a bone-shattering descent of the screes in a northerly direction towards Loch na Tuadh. This is the only foolproof way off the northern ridge of Arkle and, although it looks terrifyingly steep, it is quite safe and on the shoulder of Sail Mhor the angle relents and you reach tussocky grass.

At the west end of Loch na Tuadh you meet a stalkers' path which winds round bogs and lochans on its way to Lochstack Lodge, a grey shooting lodge overlooking the Laxford river and Loch Stack.

It is a three mile walk down the road alongside Loch Stack to Achfary but you can enjoy superb views across the loch to Arkle, while deer and buzzards can often be seen in the decaying birch woods that clothe the lower slopes of Ben Stack.

Foinaven 2999ft/908m

Start/Finish: Gualin House (305565)
Map: O.S. 1:50,000 Sheet 9
Distance: 15 miles/24km
Time: 9 hours
Grading: A tough expedition for experienced mountain walkers. Some exposed scrambling required on the ridge of A'Cheir Ghorm.

Foinaven is the undisputed queen of the Reay Forest. Its massive bulk swells up into the clouds east of Rhiconich appearing as a whaleback from the south, and its long and undulating summit ridge throws down excessively steep slopes of quartzite screes in all directions.

The shortest approach to Foinaven – from Gualin House four miles along the desolate A838 north of Rhiconich – involves a

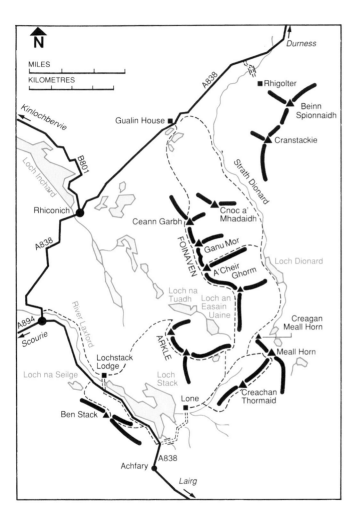

tough tramp over bog and coarse moor grass, but this route misses the wild northern corries which I consider to be the mountain's primary attraction. Thus I shall describe a longer and more complex excursion over Foinaven, which gives one of the best day's mountain walking in Scotland.

A relatively new Land Rover track runs through Strath Dionard to Loch Dionard, starting from the main road just north of Gualin House. Strath Dionard is a National Nature Reserve and the construction of the track was highly controversial because it received the blessing of the (then) Nature Conservancy Council, who considered it preferable to the appalling rutted scars in the soft peat cause by six-wheel-drive motorised buggies.

Follow this track to within a mile of Loch Dionard and enjoy the severe crags, high corries and rushing burns which descend from Foinaven's main ridge. Strath Dionard is greenshank country. Listen out for their characteristic *tew tew tew*.

Now strike up the rough bouldery hillside to the eastern abutment of the A' Cheir Ghorm ridge. This extraordinary feature thrusts out as a mile long razor-sharp spur ending abruptly in considerable cliffs. You must clamber up hideously steep slopes of quartzite scree on the south side of the crag to gain the ridge. Be warned! There is not a vestige of a path or even a footprint.

The actual crest of A' Cheir Ghorm is narrow and beset with unstable splinters of rock which can be climbed direct or circumvented. A combination of screes and cliffs fall away north and long scree gullies descend south to a grassy corrie ringed with crags.

You arrive on Foinaven's main spine at the 2845ft/867m subsidiary summit. South rises the 2644ft/806m rock prow marking the end of the ridge proper before it broadens and swoops down to the bealach under Arkle.

Walk carefully northwards across the broad expanse of sharp quartzite boulders to the large cairn on Ganu Mor, 2999ft/908m, and enjoy the view north to the breakers on the golden strand of Balnakeil Bay and west to a watery world. Lochans fill every trough and hollow and the long fingers of Lochs Inchard and Laxford penetrate far inland. It is said that on very still days a climber on Ganu Mor can hear the constant shifting of the quartzite screes.

A perfect parabolic ridge runs on to Ceann Garbh, Foinaven's northern summit, and then descends steeply to the bealach under Cnoc a'Mhadaidh. It is wise to plan your return route from this bealach, across the featureless moorland and through the inter-linked network of lochans to the cluster of trees at Gualin House.

Footnote:

In 1992 it was rumoured that the Ordnance Survey had re-surveyed Foinaven and elevated it to Munro status. This would have marked the end of Foinaven as a haven of peace and solitude but, when the facts emerged from the O.S., the spot height was confirmed as 2,999.16ft and the situation was saved. In this chapter, however, I have retained the spot height of 908m, since this is the one recorded on the current maps.

The Foinaven–Arkle Traverse

Start: Gualin House (305565)
Finish: Laxford Bridge (237467)
Map: O.S. 1:50,000 Sheet 9
Distance: 20 miles/32km
Time: 11 hours
Grading: A classic mountain day over Sutherland's grandest peaks. Mixed terrain including narrow quartzite ridges.

This is a most rewarding but energy sapping expedition which is thoroughly recommended to a fit and experienced party.

From Gualin House head south across the wide expanse of moorland, peat hags and lochans and climb Foinaven's Ceann Garbh peak via the bealach under Cnoc a'Mhadaidh.

Traverse the main ridge of Foinaven to the subsidiary summit above the A' Cheir Ghorm ridge, continue across the bealach of Cadha na Beucaich and swing east to Creag Dionard. Easy boulder fields lead down to the lowest point in the ridge above Loch an Easain Uaine which is the start of the Arkle traverse described above.

[110]

From the summit of Arkle descend the recommended route to the stalkers' path near Loch na Tuadh and follow it to Lochstack Lodge. Now take the picturesque path on the north bank of the Laxford river to the road junction at Laxford Bridge. In season you can watch the salmon at rest lying head to tail in the clear pools or flashing like silver as they leap the rapids.

Loch Stack to Gualin House

Distance: 15 miles/24km
Time: 6–7 hours

This is a highly recommended walk through the uninhabited heart of the Reay Forest. Although it does not climb above 500m, it gives exciting views into the north- and east-facing corries of Arkle and Foinaven which cannot be properly seen from the road. There is an excellent path for most of the way and route finding is no problem, but it is essential to arrange trans-port to meet you at the end of the day.

Cross the wooden bridge over the inflowing stream to Loch Stack and take the Land Rover track to the bothy of Lone. The path then climbs through a plantation at the bottom of a gully and emerges above the roaring Allt Horn.

The highest point is reached on the western shoulder of Creagan Meall Horn where the path turns eastwards and con-tinues to An Dubh Loch. Leave the stalkers' path at the loch and follow the exit stream (Allt an Easain Ghil) on the west bank as it descends to Loch Dionard.

At the north end of the loch you pick up the new track through Strath Dionard (constructed with the blessing of Scot-tish Natural Heritage because it passes through a National Nature Reserve) which leads you under the magnificent north-ern corries of Foinaven to the A838 near Gualin House.

Meall Horn 2549ft/777m

> *Start/Finish:* Achfary (296402)
> *Map:* O.S. 1:50,000 Sheet 9
> *Distance:* 11 miles
> *Time:* 6 hours
> *Grading:* An easy and rewarding walk into the heart of the Reay Forest.

Meall Horn's smoothly domed summit fills the gap between the complex convoluted hill of Meallan Liath Coire Mhic Dhughaill and the colossal quartzite massif comprising Arkle and Foinaven.

Its approach is along the Land Rover track to Lone which leaves the A838 at the south end of Loch Stack. Lone is just a locked single-storied bothy with a neighbouring cow byre and access is no problem outside the stalking season. Beyond Lone, cross the river by a wooden bridge and then branch right along a very good track above the Abhainn an Loin, which actually runs right through the hills to Gobernuisgach Lodge at the entrance to Glen Golly.

The track climbs steeply to the south shoulder of Creachan Thormaid and this outlying hill makes an interesting approach to Meall Horn because height and view are gained early. Keep as far as possible to the crest of the ridge to avoid peat hags. The going gets much easier higher up where the ground is bouldery and well drained. The south face of Creachan Thormaid has a splendid fringe of crags and these should be passed on the west side. The summit carries no cairn but there is a shallow lochan which could be useful for direction finding in mist.

Head north-east over flat boulders and grass with the rounded hump of Meall Horn directly ahead. On my ascent I saw a dotterel on this wide ridge. A short rocky descent to a bealach is necessary before making the final push to the summit of Meall Horn which is mainly grassy. To the west you look down the great corrie between Arkle and Foinaven with its two sizeable lochs, while south lies the rather gloomy Coire Ghranda with its lochan. At the end of this corrie the wide, green and featureless Strath Luib na Seilich stretches away endlessly to Bealach na Feithe.

The grassy western slopes of Meall Horn can be descended anywhere to the path beside the Allt Horn. As you turn west you enjoy views of the sharp main ridge of Foinaven and the towering east facing precipices of Arkle.

The path back to Lone is always attractive, keeping well above the Allt Horn which dashes down in a series of waterfalls and cascades. At the bottom of the gorge the path runs through a plantation of pines and exits between two enormous rocks.

The last section of the walk back to the road is alongside the shallow, reedy south end of Loch Stack, a popular spot for fishermen and red-throated divers, while beyond the loch rises the cone of Ben Stack.

Meallan Liath Coire Mhic Dhugaill 2628ft/801m

> *Start/Finish:* Kinloch (348344)
> *Map:* O.S. 1:50,000 Sheets 9, 15, 16
> *Distance:* 14 miles/22km
> *Time:* 7 hours
> *Grading:* The name is a mouthful but this is a mountain brimming with character that gives an easy and highly enjoyable day's walking.

This complex, mainly rounded mountain with umpteen corries and lochans lies south of the Foinaven-Arkle massif. The various summits are strewn with boulders of grey gneiss but the walking is easy and any cliffs and crags are well broken and can be avoided. Situated between the close-packed, chunky, knobbly hills of Glen Coul and the individual mountains of Ben Hope and Ben Loyal, it commands a wide prospect of Sutherland and even across the Pentland Firth to St John's Head on the island of Hoy.

Take the Land Rover track from Kinloch which skirts the south end of Loch More. Ben Stack looks particularly fine from here, dominating the north end of the loch and belying its mere 2365ft/721m.

At the whitewashed lodge of Aultanrynie a stalkers' path runs up behind the house on the south bank of the Allt an Reinidh, where it bears off away from the burn. Continue walking over

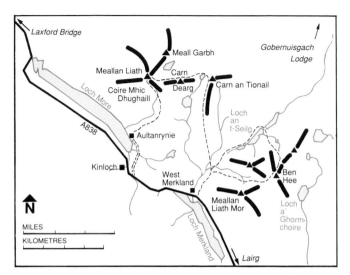

shore of Lochan a'Bhealaich. This is another of the exquisite, lonesome hill lochs on or around the Meallan Liath Coire Mhic Dhughaill massif.

Climb easily to Carn an Tionail and walk south along the broad, undulating ridge, eventually descending easy grassy slopes to the deep glen under Ben Hee which runs north to Loch an t-Seilg and Gobernuisgach Lodge.

A rather rickety suspension bridge crosses the river half a mile south of Loch an Tuim Bhuidhe. This gives access to the good track meeting the Laxford Bridge–Lairg road at West Merkland. It is now 4 km back to the car at Kinloch.

Other Worthwhile Walks

The northern outliers of Meallan Liath Coire Mhic Dhughaill can easily be climbed from Lone beside Loch Stack (see Arkle).

Follow the path eastwards through Strath Luib na Seilich to Bealach na Feithe and make an easy ascent of the rounded Meall Garbh. Continue round the rim of Blaoch Coire and descend the broad shoulder of Sail Rac to the Lone path.

The round from Achfary is 13 miles/20km and will take 6–7 hours.

Ben Hee 2864ft/873m

Start/Finish: West Merkland (384330)
Map: O.S. 1:50,000 Sheet 16
Distance: 9 miles/14km
Time: 4–5 hours
Grading: An easy expedition up a mainly grassy mountain.

Driving south from Laxford Bridge to Loch Shin and Lairg, you pass beneath a long range of high mountains: Arkle, Meall Horn, Meallan Liath Coire Mhic Dhughaill and Ben Hee.

Arkle, with its cliffs and corries of quartzite, clearly belongs with Foinaven but the last three named mountains are folded, mainly bare and grassy with few dramatic features.

Ben Hee's swelling mounds can be glimpsed from the north

rough grass and hags into the wide upper corrie. Meallan Liath Coire Mhic Dhughaill can be seen rising ahead with some low crags on the west side. It is simple enough to ascend directly to the bouldery summit, where I surprised two mountain hares and a family of ptarmigan. The O.S. pillar stands snugly inside a protecting wall.

Well defined ridges branch out in all directions like spokes of a wheel and dozens of tempting walks are possible from this focal point. Away to the north-west Arkle sits squatly like a suet pudding but it is Ben Hope's superb west-facing cliffs which catch the attention.

To avoid straying further into the mountain wilderness of Sutherland, take the south-east ridge to the pronounced cairn on Carn Dearg. This overlooks Loch Ulbhach Coire with its sizeable lake and line of crags, Creag na h-Uidhe. However, this corrie does not look inviting to visit because of its vast area of peat hags and it is preferable to continue eastwards and descend quite steeply, stepwise, with some rocks to avoid, to reach the end of Loch Merkland, and this is the best starting point for an ascent of the mountain which should make a not too taxing day under most conditions.

From the road bridge at West Merkland walk up the Land Rover track which runs north all the way to Gobernuisgach Lodge, Glen Golly and Strath More. After a mile, at a wooden bridge, turn sharp eastwards along a narrow path beside the Allt Coir' a'Chruiteir. Height is quickly gained and when the path peters out high up the shallow corrie under Ben Hee a line of cairns guide you to the shoulder above Coire nam Mang. Flat grey stones litter the summit of Ben Hee and craggy slopes descend steeply on the east side to a group of lochans.

Descend north-east to reach the bealach under the un-named subsidiary summit across the corrie which is characterised by a prominent cliff above the bealach. A landslip has produced some unusual trenches on the broad and grassy ridge.

Continue the descent northwards from the bealach down a boulder field to a picturesque lochan in the corrie. Throughout the descent the monolithic Ben Hope dominates the view down the glen. Now follow the lochan exit stream, Allt a'Gharbh-choire, to the narrow spit of land dividing Loch an Aslaird from Loch an t-Seilig. The connecting stream is crossed by a line of huge stepping stones enabling you to reach the main track again, about three miles from West Merkland.

Meallan Liath Coire Mhic Dhughaill, a complex and convoluted mountain in the Reay Forest, is seen here from the west. Photo: Tom Rix.

11 THE FAR NORTH

North-west of Foinaven lies a desolate wasteland of wet and tussocky moorland. This area is called the Parph and it is almost completely devoid of habitation. Few walkers brave the trackless bogs to climb the rather nondescript hills of Creag Riabhach and Fashven which rise to nearly 1600ft/500m.

Although the Parph can be enjoyed for its rather special character and far from obvious attributes, its coastline is universally acclaimed as magnificent. In the chapter on coastal walks I have described both the walks south from Cape Wrath via Sandwood Bay to Oldshoremore and east to Bay of Kearvaig. The former in particular is a must. Visitors can rejoice that the encompassing estate has been bought, and will be sensitively managed for the nation, by the John Muir Trust.

East of the Parph the fine ridges on Cranstackie and Beinn Spionnaidh give wonderful views over Loch Eriboll, while the most northerly Munro, Ben Hope, possesses many dramatic rock features and overlooks the woods beside Loch Hope. From Ben Hope you can look east across the Pentland Firth to the Isle of Hoy and south to the long line of grassy mountains comprising Meall Horn, Meallan Liath Coire Mhic Dhughaill and Ben Hee.

A few miles further east, and just south of the Kyle of Tongue, rises one of Scotland's most beautiful mountains. Ben Loyal thrusts four granite peaks into the sky and, rising from sea level, can proudly take its place amongst the other undisputed gems of Sutherland: Suilven, Quinag and Foinaven.

Ben Loyal, one of the most northerly mountains in Britain, rises high above the village of Tongue. Photo: Jim Teesdale.

Cranstackie 2625ft/800m and Beinn Spionnaidh 2533ft/772m

Start/Finish: A838 near turn-off to Rhigolter (332592)
Map: O.S. 1:50,000 Sheet 9
Distance: 8 miles/12km
Time: 5 hours
Grading: An easy walk over two individual hills which provide wonderful views over the far north-west.

These two very graceful hills rise north of Strath Dionard and extend nearly to the Kyle of Durness. Their rounded shoulders are the perfect complement to the savage north facing cliffs of Foinaven and they can give a most pleasant walk right on the northern tip of Britain, with fine views over the sands of the Kyle and to the shimmering blue waters of Loch Eriboll.

The natural route over these hills would be from Strath Dionard in the south but my attempt was foiled by an inability to cross the foaming river Dionard, which rises quickly after rain. An approach from the south is thus virtually precluded, except in very dry weather. However, there is a bridge over the river Dionard at the farm of Rhigolter, three miles north of Gualin House, and a perfectly satisfactory circular route can be accomplished from there.

Leave the car on the A838 and walk down the rough road to the bridge and whitewashed farmhouse of Rhigolter. Beinn Spionnaidh throws out a prominent ridge to the west which ends in a grassy knob above Rhigolter. This provides an easy, though steep, route of ascent. Near the top of the mountain, grassy slopes give way to a boulder-strewn plateau with a substantial cairn. The O.S. trig pillar stands 300m to the north of this cairn.

Return to the subsidiary cairn and then descend more boulders for about 500ft/150m to reach the grassy bealach under Cranstackie. The ascent to Cranstackie is up a broad stony ridge, supported by a line of low and rather broken crags, which leads to two more well built cairns.

Enjoy the wonderful views south into the corries of Foinaven and then retrace your steps to the bealach, whence the open, grassy corrie leads you back down to Rhigolter Farm.

Ben Hope 3041ft/927m

> Start/Finish: Altnacaillich (457456)
> Map: O.S. 1:50,000 Sheet 9
> Distance: 10 miles/16km
> Time: 6–7 hours
> Grading: A good path leads to the summit by the tourist route. Some rock scrambling involved on the north ridge if the complete traverse is to be achieved

The great mountains of the far north-west tend to rise abruptly from the bedrock and Ben Hope is no exception. The mountain, which is the most northerly Munro, stands proudly at the south end of Loch Hope just a few miles from Scotland's north coast. Its west facing precipices, which rise above lower slopes that are pleasantly wooded with birch, are seamed by lines of buttresses and gullies, giving it an air of impregnability when viewed from Foinaven, Arkle or Meallan Liath Coire Mhic Dhughaill. Yet the tiered southern slopes are easy angled and, together with a well beaten path, they make Ben Hope a popular objective for holiday visitors.

A quick ascent can be made from the minor road running between Altnaharra and Hope on the A838. Two kilometres north of Altnacaillich a waymark indicates the start of an excellent path which climbs steeply to the broad south shoulder of Ben Hope. Near the top a line of cairns guide you to the O.S. trig pillar which is set back from the cliffs.

If you have more time, a complete south to north traverse of Ben Hope makes a much more worthwhile day. For this expedition take the path from Altnacaillich along the south side of the burn which passes some waterfalls before ascending gently to Leitir Mhuiseil and the upper terrace of Ben Hope.

The descent down the north ridge is steep, sharp and rocky and is best left to those with rock climbing experience. The crux is an exposed 30ft step which can be avoided by a scrambly route on the east side. Continue the descent westwards, passing Dubh-loch na Beinne, to reach the road at the head of Loch Hope just 5km north of Altnacaillich.

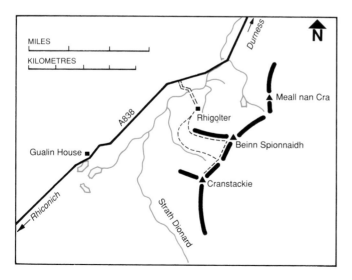

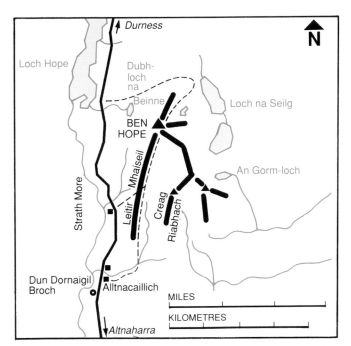

N.B. Just south of Altnacaillich stands Dun Dornaigil, a splendid Pictish broch. Brochs were built at the turn of the Christian era as defended homesteads. Dun Dornaigil has walls 22ft high and 14ft thick

Ben Loyal 2506ft/764m

Start/Finish: Ribigill (582542)
Map: O.S. 1:50,000 Sheet 10
Distance: 9 miles/14km
Time: 5–6 hours
Grading: A straightforward ascent of a most beautiful mountain. Some exposed scrambling which can be avoided if necessary.

Ben Loyal divides the rough, harsh, quartzite mountains of the Reay Forest from the flat, saturated moorlands of the Flow Country of eastern Sutherland. Its combination of shapely summits, narrow but rounded ridges, bold crags, smoothly sculptured corries, lochans, gorges and wooded slopes not only gladdens the eye but provides the hill walker with a day of extravagant pleasures. The inherent characteristics of Ben Loyal can best be appreciated from the Kyle of Tongue to the northwest, whence it is considered by many to be the perfect Scottish mountain.

From the village of Tongue, an unfenced road runs south off the A838 to Kinloch Lodge at the head of the Kyle of Tongue. Park near Ribigill Farm and follow the muddy track south to the shieling of Cunside. Throughout this two-mile approach you are presented with a magnificent view of the triangular north face of Sgor Chaonasaid, a lesser Buachaille Etive Mor.

Skirt the steepest section of the face to the east and scramble up ledgy, broken ground and some damp, mossy gullies to the sharp summit. Descend a short distance to a bealach and then climb to the rocky twin summits of Sgor a'Bhatain. This involves the traverse of a narrow granite crest but it can be avoided on the east side if necessary.

Cross a marshy plateau to the vast rock tooth of An Caisteal, the true summit, where there is a grey stone O.S. trig pillar and some pools in depressions in the rocks. The summit tooth has sheer faces on the south and east sides and care is needed in mist. But in clear weather you can look to Ben Hope, Ben More Assynt, the folded hill of Meallan Liath Coire Mhic Dhughaill and other mountains of the Reay Forest. The watery wastes of

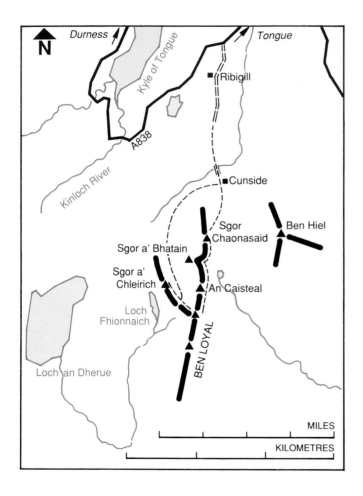

the Flow Country, Loch Loyal, Loch Eriboll, the Pentland Firth and the distant cliffs of St John's Head on Hoy stretch out below.

Keep to the broad summits surrounding the shallow, unnamed north-facing corrie and make for the prominent rock nose of Sgor a'Chleirich above Loch Fhionnaich. Retrace your steps south to the bealach and scramble down grassy slopes into the corrie, whence the burn guides you down through the decayed woods of Coille na Cuile to the bare moorland. Your line of descent takes you under towering buttresses of clean rock thrown down from Sgor a'Bhatain and you emerge on lower ground at a collection of ruined crofts.

Looking across the Kyle of Tongue from Ben Loyal. Photo: Tom Rix.

12 COASTAL WALKS

The coastline between Kyle of Lochalsh and Cape Wrath, and then east to the Kyle of Tongue, has a great diversity of character but is universally extremely rough. Rocks, skerries, shingle, boulders, broad strands, coves, caves, blow-holes, arches, cliffs and stacks can all be seen.

Unlike much of Britain, cliff-top and coastal paths are almost unknown in the Far North West but almost every stretch of coastline is worth visiting. Although access can be difficult because of the nature of the ground the rewards are commensurate.

In this chapter I have described some of my favourite coastal walks. All have impressive features and can be enjoyed even in stormy weather when mountains make unsuitable objectives.

Applecross Peninsula. Toscaig to Airigh-drishaig

Distance: 10 miles/16km
Time: 6 hours

Although a new road now runs round the west and north sides of the Applecross peninsula, providing a lifeline to the coastal settlements of Kalnakill, Cuaig and Fearnmore, the southern tip remains isolated and deserted.

A wild and rugged walk can be made from the road-end at Toscaig, round the southern tip of Applecross, Rubha na h-Uamha, to the old crofting settlement at Airigh-drishaig. Four miles of boggy track then lead back to Toscaig over peaty hills

Kearvaig Bay, three miles east of Cape Wrath, with its twin off-shore stacks. Photo: Richard Gilbert.

with sandstone outcrops and lonely lochans. The coastal section is a tough, trackless walk through thick heather and coarse grass with much ascent and descent necessary to overcome cliffs and ravines. It is not suitable for families with young children.

Park near the jetty at Toscaig and cross the river where it fans out on the stony beach. The line of an old path can be seen rising from the beach and making for the headland, but it is little more than a sheep trod and it soon disappears.

The easiest ground lies well back from the shore and you pass a grassy patch with some tumble-down walls and piles of stone, a pathetic effort by crofters to clear some ground for grazing or lazy-bedding. A mile away across the sound, Caolas Mor, the Crowlin islands look very fine.

The next point of interest is the area of thick oak woodlands surrounding the inlet just before Uags. Over the next brow lies Uags itself, a collection of three or four cottages and cow-sheds. All are ruined save one cottage with a roof which could provide a little shelter.

Ahead lie three rough miles before you can descend to the woods at Airigh-drishaig. Oaks predominate, mingled with birch, alder and holly.

After so much wild country it is amazing to find a ramshackle bridge over the burn near another group of crofts. Surprisingly a tiny whitewashed cottage is inhabited, vegetables grow in a walled garden and a Heath Robinson hydro scheme provides some power. The position is magnificent, looking right across the island-studded mouth of Loch Kishorn into Loch Carron.

The path back to Toscaig roughly follows a line of poles carrying electricity to Applecross, a lower and less exposed route than the Bealach na Ba.

Diabaig to Redpoint

> **Distance:** 7 miles/11km
> **Time:** 4 hours

The narrow road running west from Torridon village ends at the tiny harbour and settlement of Lower Diabaig, which looks

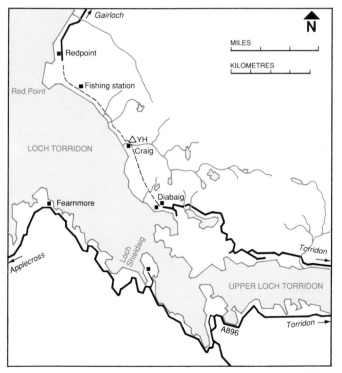

MILES

KILOMETRES

The deserted crofting settlement at Uags on the wild Applecross coast with Dun Caan on Raasay just visible in the background. Photo: Richard Gilbert.

across the mouth of Loch Torridon to the northern point of the Applecross peninsula.

Although another road hugs the coastline south of Gairloch it stops at Redpoint, just seven miles short of Diabaig but, if transport can be arranged, the connection can be made on foot. A well marked path which keeps right to the water's edge for much of the way gives a fascinating walk with lovely views to Skye and Raasay, and it passes the remote Youth Hostel at Craig. This stretch of coast is rich in wild life with sea birds, waders, otters and a herd of wild goats.

From the road end at the western extremity of Lower Diabaig the path keeps some way above the sea as it crosses the shoulder of Sidhein a'Mhill. It is rather boggy but cairns mark the best route.

After two miles you descend to the Craig River which is lined with birch trees and you should follow the river bank downstream from the Youth Hostel to a bridge.

The next few miles keep close to the coastline climbing above cliffs and fording numerous streams. A sandy bay is reached just before a fishing station with huts and long poles on which nets are hung to dry. Dunes and fields lead to Redpoint Farm with the car park and viewpoint just beyond.

Camus Mor

> **Distance:** 4 miles/6km
> **Time:** 3–4 hours

A magnificently wild and rocky coastline runs along the north side of the Rubha Reidh peninsula which thrusts out into the Minch between Loch Gairloch and Loch Ewe.

The secluded, sandy inlet of Camus Mor, which is very difficult of access, exemplifies this stretch of splintered coast and makes an exciting objective.

The walk starts from the Rubha Reidh lighthouse but, unless you obtain permission to drive along the three miles of private road north of Melvaig, you must allow for an extra two hours and six miles.

Although the easiest way across the peat-hagged hillside to Camus Mor takes a line well above the cliff-top, it is well worth hugging the coastline for the first mile. This is to marvel at three superb rock stacks (two graceful needles and one massive block) which rise high above the waves just off-shore from a bouldery beach.

Inevitably you are forced higher and higher to round a line of cliffs before you can descend steeply to the wide sandy bay of Camus Mor. The bay is sheltered by high promontories on either side while slopes of cropped grass run back from the high tide line. Driftwood abounds and it is a perfect place for a picnic.

Black Bay and Eilean Furadh Mor

Distance: 3 miles/5km
Time: 2 hours

The road up the east side of the Rubha Reidh peninsula stops one mile beyond the village of Cove at some concrete slabs used in World War Two as gun emplacements. From this point a rough walk westwards along the indented coastline for one-and-a-half miles, passing two low rocky islets, brings you to Black Bay which is directly opposite the grassy Eilean Furadh Mor.

In fine weather this is an idyllic spot where I have lunched to the cries of oyster catchers and the eerie groaning of seals on the skerries lying off the island which is barely 300m away.

Two rusty lifeboats cast up on the rocks bear witness to one of the worst ever disasters on the west coast of Scotland. On the night of February 24th 1944 a convoy was entering Loch Ewe when the American Liberty ship *William H. Welsh* was dashed onto the tip of Eilean Furadh Mor. It was a pitch black night of storm, snow and tempestuous seas and the ship soon broke into two pieces.

There was little alternative but for the crew to attempt to make for the safety of the shore through the breaking waves. In spite of heroic efforts by the local community from Cove, who battled in atrocious conditions throughout the next day, only

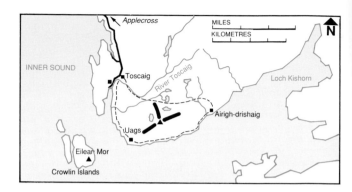

twelve men survived the wreck from a crew of seventy four, while forty bodies were never recovered.

On a still summer day it is hard to imagine those desperate scenes over fifty years ago; you need to have experienced a full-scale winter's storm for the full horror to be brought home.

Badrallach to Scoraig

Distance: 10 miles/16km
Time: 5 hours

Loch Broom is always busy and bustling with the Altnaharrie ferry, the Stornoway car ferry, fishing boats, factory ships, yachts, canoes, power boats and water skiing. But Little Loch Broom to the south, over the shoulder of Beinn Ghobhlach, is peaceful and beautiful. A narrow path runs along its northern shore, providing a gentle and attractive walk, particularly on a summer evening.

From Dundonnell drive along the minor road to Badrallach where the road ends at the tiny settlement which is little more than a string of cottages, a post office and telephone. The path starts immediately, and for five miles meanders above the shoreline through heather and bracken giving close-up views of the beach and its associated wild life.

The path ends at Scoraig, an interesting community that is served irregularly by a ferry from Badluarach across Little Loch Broom. Scoraig looks south across the loch to the huge mass of Sail Mhor and to An Teallach. About twenty years ago there was an influx of families to Scoraig. They took over ruined crofts and occupied themselves with crofting and many different cottage industries.

Rather than return to Badrallach the same way, an energetic party can climb the shapely Beinn Ghobhlach which is the best viewpoint of all for the Summer Isles. The route takes the high ground eastwards to meet the road near Loch na h-Airbhe. (A more detailed description is found in the ascent of Beinn Ghobhlach which I have placed in the Great Wilderness chapter.)

The Rubha Coigeach Peninsula. Reiff to Achnahaird Bay

> *Distance: 10 miles/16km*
> *Time: 5 hours*

This rough and mainly trackless walk goes right round the Rubha Coigeach peninsula which makes up the southern arm of Enard Bay. The coastline is characterised by sandstone cliffs, bays of shingle and boulders, very wild and boggy moorland and numerous off-shore islets and skerries. The cliffs are becoming increasingly popular with rock climbers and the entire peninsula is rich in bird life, On one recent walk we saw all three types of diver: red throated, black throated and great northern. Seals can often be seen in the secluded bays.

Park at Reiff, cross the exit stream of the sea loch by a gated bridge and walk across cropped grass to the beach. The cliffs become more pronounced as you walk north and you soon reach a stone-built wind-shelter on a minor headland. I remember sheltering here one winter's day when the wind was storm force and spume was blowing clean over the top of the cliffs. It was all we could do to raise our heads above the parapet. On such days this coastline is awe inspiring, such is the noise and strength of the waves pounding the shore.

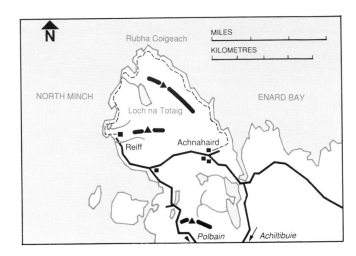

After rounding Faochag Bay the cliffs rise again and form a prominent overhanging prow. Shags can be seen in lines on the skerries, stretching our their wings to dry, and fulmars nest on the ledges.

As you round the point and head south, the coastline becomes increasingly indented and in several places you have to make considerable detours inland to round gullies and blow-holes. But the rewards are spectacular with views north to Stoer lighthouse, Suilven and the islands of Enard Bay.

Eventually you reach the broad sandy bay at Achnahaird. It is sadly overlooked by a caravan site but I once saw a stranded minke whale there. Unless you are prepared for a four mile walk back along the road to Reiff you should arrange transport to meet you at Achnahaird.

Stoer Lighthouse to the Old Man

> *Distance: 3–4 miles/5km*
> *Time: 2 hours*

The white painted Stoer lighthouse is a well-known landmark, visible from many of the hills of Coigach and Assynt and even from An Teallach on a clear day.

A narrow road which serves a number of tiny crofting communities branches north from the Lochinver to Drumbeg road near Stoer; it ends at a car park adjacent to the lighthouse. A stretch of wild, cliff-girt coastline runs north for about two miles and the undercut 200ft rock stack known as the Old Man of Stoer rises just off shore. The Old Man makes an interesting objective for a leisurely picnic or a half-day excursion.

A rather wet path follows the edge of the cliffs, swooping and diving in and out of gullies, for about a mile and a half until the Old Man is reached. On the top of the cliffs, a flat grassy platform, speckled with flowers, makes a good viewpoint for the stack, the bird life and the waves pounding the rocks. If the tide is low, to ease the crossing of the foaming gulf to reach the stack, you may see rock climbers at work for an ascent of the Old Man is a popular challenge.

An alternative and somewhat easier return route climbs to the cairn on the summit of Sidhean Mor, the high point on the moor behind the Old Man. You should then head south to pick up a path which passes a collection of derelict Nissen huts on its way back to the lighthouse.

Handa Island

Distance: 3 miles/5km
Time: 3 hours

Handa Island is a nature reserve and bird reserve, administered by the RSPB, situated off the Sutherland coast just north of Scourie. Visitors are welcome provided they keep to the paths and, during the summer months, a small, open ferry boat operates several times a day from Tarbet on the mainland, crossing the Sound of Handa and running straight onto the sandy shore.

Handa is a beautiful and romantic island with plunging cliffs and a wild coastline. It is the nesting ground for many thousands of sea birds. I thoroughly recommend it to visitors but, before leaving for Tarbet, they should check that the ferry is running by phoning 01971 502340.

Close by the landing bay there is an old graveyard for, before the clearances, Handa was occupied by twelve families. A rather boggy path, partially alleviated by duck-boards, runs across the island to the north coast. Quite suddenly the ground drops away dramatically, leaving you on the edge of a sheer cliff with the waves breaking on a boulder-strewn beach 300ft below.

Follow the path west to the Great Stack, a massive pillar of red sandstone completely detached from the main cliff. If you sit on the cliff-top in early summer you will be deafened by the screaming of thousands of birds and mesmerised by their aerobatics as they swoop and glide, effortlessly riding the up-draughts.

Puffins nest in burrows on the very top of the stack, while the

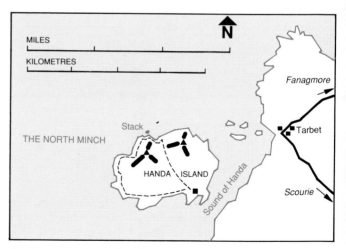

Rough seas pound magnificent Sandwood Bay six miles south of Cape Wrath. Photo: Ian Evans.

ledges below make nesting sites for upwards of 12,000 birds, mainly guillemots and razorbills. Fulmars, too, contest the sites while the air is thick with kittiwakes and greater black backed gulls. Shags sit in rows on the off-shore skerries. Great skuas (bonxies) nest on the moorland of Handa and commonly dive-bomb visitors. The resident RSPB warden on Handa walks around in a workman's hard hat!

The west coast of Handa gives marvellous coastal views north to the cliffs of Cape Wrath and south to the Point of Stoer. The path along the cliffs passes close to some blow-holes where the sea booms and rumbles far below. Then the cliffs give way to a low rocky shore before the path heads back inland to complete the circuit.

Oldshoremore to Cape Wrath

Distance: 16 miles/26km
Time: 8 hours

Gale lashed, pounded remorselessly by Atlantic rollers, and virtually uninhabited, the coastline south of Cape Wrath offers the walker an exhilarating and memorable experience. Here are found sheer cliffs of gneiss and sandstone, skerries and islets sending the waves into columns of spray with a clap of thunder, wheeling, screaming sea-birds and wide sandy bays. By a considerable margin this is the finest coastal walk described in this book and many people rate Sandwood Bay the most magnificent bay to be found in the whole of Britain. In 1993 the Sandwood Estate, which includes the coastline from Oldshoremore to the north of Sandwood Bay, was bought for the nation by the John Muir Trust to protect its wild nature.

Before setting out on this expedition, which runs from Oldshoremore to Cape Wrath, be sure to phone 01971 511376 to check the times of the minibus and ferry that will take you from the lighthouse to the Cape Wrath Hotel at Kyle of Durness. The alternative is an extra sixteen miles of walking at the end of an already very arduous day.

Start from the car park by the burial ground at Oldshoremore and proceed northwards, hugging the coastline wherever possible. At times you descend to hidden coves where you will startle oyster catchers and at other times you traverse round hillocks on heather moorland and eroded peat.

At Port Mor a stack of rock thrusts skyward, topped by an extraordinary ovoid stone, covered with yellow lichen (*Xanthoria parietina*) like the egg of a prehistoric bird. Further on, as you draw level with the island group of Am Balg, the cliffs rise to 400ft and, if you peer over the edge, you will see the famous pinnacle of Am Buachaille (the herdsman) rising 220ft above the waves. It was first climbed by Tom Patey's party in 1967.

Rounding the cliff beyond Am Buachaille, one of the most glorious sights in Britain unfolds. Below your feet lies Sandwood Bay, a mile-long sweep of golden sand bounded by rolling dunes and crashing breakers that make you want to shout for joy.

Spend a few minutes watching the gannets diving for fish, and then climb to the cliff-top on the north side of the bay. Look back at lonely Sandwood Loch, the cottage beyond the dunes and the tidal islands where legends tell us mermaids play. A Spanish galleon, fleeing after the Armada debacle, is rumoured to have foundered offshore and the wreck, including treasure, buried in the sands. A surviving mariner haunts the lonely cottage where, on wild nights, visitors have reported hearing knocking at the window and seeing a swarthy, bearded sailor in cap, tunic with brass buttons and seaboots, and displaying long gold earrings, peering into the room.

The last six miles to Cape Wrath are exceptionally tough as you switchback from cliff-top to bouldery beach, but the scenery becomes even more dramatic. Waves boom through caves and blow-holes, spray leaps from the shattered rocks and a natural arch runs through the headland at Bay of Keisgaig. Watch out for great skuas (bonxies) which dive-bomb unsuspecting visitors.

Cape Wrath lighthouse and the accompanying cottages come as an anticlimax; man-made structures are incongruous in a natural environment of such grandeur.

Sandwood Bay

If you just wish to visit Sandwood Bay, without including it in the Cape Wrath Coastal Walk, you only need to walk 5 or 6 miles (there and back).

Drive to Kinlochbervie and then take the minor road north through Oldshoremore to the crofting settlement of Blairmore. Here a very rough, but drivable road, runs north to just past Loch na Gainimh where there are several parking places.

Walk on to Loch a'Mhuillinn where you skirt the water's edge on firm sand to reach a cairned path that takes you to Sandwood Bay. The path traverses the hillside above Lochs Meadhonach and Clais nan Coinneal where you should look out for divers.

Be warned, bathing is not advised at Sandwood Bay because of currents and a very strong undertow.

Cape Wrath to Kearvaig Bay

Distance: 4 miles/6km
Time: 2–3 hours

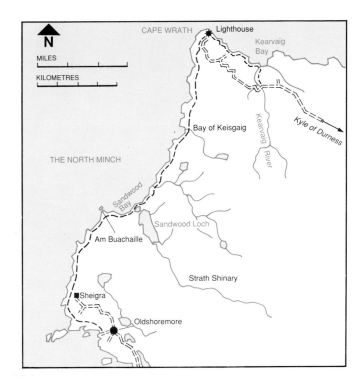

I have written enthusiastically about the cliff-top walk north to Cape Wrath from Oldshoremore via Sandwood Bay; another fascinating coastal walk can be enjoyed by heading east along the very northernmost edge of Britain.

Again you must take the little ferryboat across the Kyle of Durness and the rickety minibus across the desolate Parph to Cape Wrath lighthouse. There is no path along the cliffs heading east and you must take care to keep well back from the edge where the grass can be wet and slippery.

After a rough and boggy mile you descend to a tiny inlet where large oil tanks supply fuel for the lighthouse, then up again to the peat hags and some tiny lochans before you drop down to Kearvaig Bay.

Your response to the beauty and grandeur of Kearvaig Bay when you round the headland and see it for the first time is akin to the feelings engendered by your first glimpse of Sandwood Bay. A wide sweep of perfect sand fills the bay which is bounded by towering cliffs. Rocky spurs run out into the sea, huge twin stacks holding a giant chockstone rise on the east side while to the west you can see clear daylight through rock arches which jut out from Cape Wrath itself. A large stream, the Kearvaig river, cuts through the sand on its way to the sea and it must be waded or boulder hopped.

On my last visit Cape Wrath was cold and windy with a thin, wet mist enveloping the lighthouse whose foghorn was booming. Two hours later we ran out across the firm sand at Kearvaig Bay with the sun shining from a blue sky and fulmars

and great skuas (bonxies) circling the cliffs; we were elated at the wildness of the scene before us.

An empty cottage stands above the high water mark whence a track runs back up the hill to the road where you can rendezvous with the Kyle of Durness minibus.

East of Kearvaig Bay there is an RAF bombing range; the off-shore island of An Garbh-eilean is used as a target. When the range is in use, sentries bar the road, even for the minibus, and there is no question of continuing the walk. But when the range is not being used you can walk along the top of the stupendous Clo Mor cliffs (the highest on the mainland of Britain) and reach the road again at Achiemore.

Faraid Head

> *Distance: 4 miles/6km*
> *Time: 2 hours*

Faraid Head is a promontory of close-cropped grass, machair, marram and sand dunes. It runs north for two miles from Balnakeil.

Take the road signed to the golf course from Durness and park near the ruined church and burial ground at the south end of Balnakeil Bay.

Walk across the beautiful sandy bay to an old road, part tarmac, part concrete but mainly drifted over with sand. This runs north to the Ministry of Defence lookout point where observations are made of the bombing practice on An Garbh-eilean which can be seen off-shore.

While the west side of the head is sandy, the east is cliff-girt with islets, rocks and skerries emerging above the waves. You can skirt the fenced area to reach the grassy north-west finger of Faraid Head, an idyllic spot in summer with views across the Kyle of Durness to Foinaven and south-east to Ben Hope and Ben Loyal.

The Old Man of Stoer, a 200-foot sandstone pinnacle which provides a severe challenge to rock climbers. Photo: Ken Bryan.

Opposite: *At low tide a broad sweep of sand at Balnakeil Bay extends northwards towards Faraid Head. Photo: Richard Gilbert.*

13 SANDY BAYS

Families who are looking for a day on a sandy beach may find this list useful, although in some cases sand only appears when the tide is out. The bays are listed in order from south to north and then east from Cape Wrath. They can all be easily identified from the O.S. 1:50,000 scale map. The reference is given alongside.

Camus Dubh-aird (near Plockton airstrip) (787333)
Loch Reraig (near Ardaneaskan) (837362)
Applecross (715455)
Sand (683487)
Cuaig (705586)
Annat (895544)
Red Point (north and south) (728688) and (735674)
Gairloch (800771)
Big Sand (752786)
Camus Mor (758918)
Mellangaun (812897)
Firemare (818882)

Aultbea (870892)
Slaggan (840941) (walk in three miles across moorland from Achgarve to this lonely bay)
Opinan (883970)
Mellon Udrigle (890958)
Laide (902920)
Gruinard (951899)
Achnahaird (020125)
Achmelvich (055249)
Clachtoll (040271)
Clashnessie (056309)
Scourie (150447)
Oldshoremore (197586)
Sandwood (220655)
Kearvaig (290728)
Balnakeil (392695)
Sango (408677)
Ceannabeinne (443656)

The Coigach peaks seen across Achnahaird Bay. Left to right: Stac Pollaidh, Cul Beag and Beinn an Eoin. Photo: Alan O'Brien.

14 PLACES OF INTEREST. HISTORIC SITES. HOUSES AND GARDENS

The Kyle Line

The Inverness to Kyle of Lochalsh railway opened in 1870. It is a triumph of Victorian engineering and throughout its 82 miles it passes through some of Scotland's most beautiful and dramatic scenery. I can highly recommend it to visitors.

Three trains run in each direction every weekday and Saturday (but none on Sunday) and the mid-morning train, which arrives at Kyle for lunch, allows you nearly four hours in the village before returning. (Enough time for a quick trip over to Skye!) The train can be picked up at Dingwall or Garve if required.

The scenery is entrancing, especially when seen from a special observation coach, and much better than that experienced by road travel. Watch out for tree-ringed Loch Garve, Loch Luichart, a glimpse of the Torridon hills from Achnasheen, the woods of Achnashellach, Loch Carron and the Coulin Forest hills, the ruins of Strome Castle, the Applecross hills, Duncraig Castle set amongst rhododendrons, the harbour and cottages at Plockton, the rocky coastline beyond Duirinish with views west to the islands of Raasay, Scalpay, Longay, Pabay and the Crowlins and, of course, the distant outline of the Cuillins of Skye.

Plockton

This extremely attractive village a few miles north of Kyle of Lochalsh looks across a group of tiny islands to the mouth of Loch Carron. The hinterland is well wooded and provides many delightful short walks. Plockton offers a number of good hotels and shops. Fishing and sailing trips can be arranged.

Plockton, a peaceful village and popular holiday centre in a sheltered inlet of Loch Carron. Photo: Gordon Gadsby.

Applecross

This village on the west coast of the vast Applecross peninsula seems almost completely cut off from mainland Scotland. Yet it is the centre for a number of tiny communities strung out along the coast. There is a post office, general store, hotel, home bakery, tea room, camp site and a number of bed and breakfast establishments. Fishing trips can be arranged.

The whitewashed cottages overlook the bay that has a wide stretch of sand at low tide. Mature beech and sycamore trees ring the bay above the high-water mark.

Lochcarron

A pretty village strung out alongside Loch Carron which can offer visitors golf, sailing and, at North Strome, a trip round Loch Carron Weavers which is open on weekdays throughout the year.

Beside the Kishorn river at Rassal, west of Lochcarron, is Britain's most northerly ash wood, where limestone outcrops have encouraged a fascinating flora and a rich bird life. Rassal is a Nature Reserve but is open to the public.

Shieldaig

Shieldaig is perhaps the most popular showpiece village in Wester Ross. A crescent of whitewashed cottages stands back from a sheltered bay on the south side of Loch Torridon. Colourful boats bob at their moorings or are pulled up onto the shingle beach. A wooded island, owned by the National Trust for Scotland, stands just off-shore. Shieldaig has a hotel, several bed and breakfast establishments, a post-office and a general store.

Torridon

National Trust for Scotland Countryside Centre with information on the Torridon area, a red deer museum and an audio visual display on wildlife. Open May to the end of September.

The Beinn Eighe National Nature Reserve

The National Nature Reserve on Beinn Eighe is one of the most important and impressive in Britain. It was the first to be established in Britain, in 1951, and it has won an international reputation. Nowadays it is run by Scottish Natural Heritage.

Situated south of Loch Maree, the reserve covers 4,800 hectares and its main purpose is to conserve the remnant Scots pine forest, Coille na Glas Leitire on the lower slopes of Beinn Eighe. But the reserve has much more to offer: classical geological structures, glacial landforms, a great diversity of habitats for wild life and a distinctive flora.

The wonderful woodlands and the classic geological features of different mountain zones are best experienced at first hand by walking the four mile Beinn Eighe Mountain Trail, which starts at a car park on the A832 three miles north of Kinlochewe. This trail is described in the account of the ascent of Meall a'Ghiubhais.

If it is not possible to walk the trail, you should spend some time at the Reserve Visitor's Centre which is on the roadside just one mile north of Kinlochewe. Here you can see photographs and exhibits which will give you some idea of the character of the reserve and the fauna which live there.

The Fairy Lochs War Grave

In June 1945 a USAAF B-24H Liberator took off from Prestwick to return to America via Iceland. In thick mist it struck the summit rocks of Slioch but managed to fly on towards Gairloch, finally crashing into the hillside beside the Fairy Lochs above Shieldaig.

Shieldaig (not to be confused with the Shieldaig beside Loch Torridon) lies four miles south of Gairloch on the Badachro road. The crash site is now a War Grave and it can be visited by a short walk of about two miles there and back. Allow one-and-a-half hours.

Park just west of the Shieldaig Lodge Hotel and take the Land Rover track that runs south past a farm, heading to Loch Braigh Horrisdale. After a short distance turn left at a cairn and ascend the boggy hillside to the Fairy Lochs. There is a well marked path.

The wreckage and remembrance tablet are situated in a very quiet and beautiful spot beside a small loch whose waves gently lap the shore at ref. 808711. A twisted propeller blade mounted in a rock sums up the appalling tragedy in which the crew of nine and all six passengers lost their lives.

Gairloch

Gairloch is a large village with good shops and communications and plenty of accommodation. There is golf, fishing and windsurfing for visitors.

Gairloch Heritage Museum is situated in a former farmstead built round a cobbled courtyard. Exhibits have been chosen to record life in and around Gairloch from prehistoric times.

A gallery attached to the museum shows the history of the Gaels and there is an adjoining restaurant. The Gairloch Museum is open Monday to Saturday between Easter and September.

Cove Cave

Near the middle of the tiny village of Cove, a line of posts with yellow marker discs leads you across a field to the seashore and a remarkable cave.

The low cave runs far into the cliff just above the high water line. It is gloomy and grotto-like with water dripping from the roof, but it was once fitted out with a wooden floor, altar, pulpit and pews and used as a church.

Inverewe Gardens

These gardens, constructed during the life time of Sir Osgood Mackenzie on a spit of land jutting out into Loch Ewe just north of Poolewe, are now owned by the National Trust for Scotland

and are justifiably one of the top tourist attractions in Scotland.

The benign influence of the gulf stream means that 2,500 species can flourish in an area of only 64 acres. Thus, early rhododendrons come into flower in February or March.

Osgood Mackenzie bought the estate in 1862 and worked until his death in 1922 to transform it into the world renowned gardens that they are today. His daughter Mrs Mairi Sawyer continued her father's work for another 30 years before handing them over to the NTS.

Gruinard Bay

A visit to Gruinard Bay is a must for any traveller to Wester Ross.

This sheltered, sandy and wide inlet gets the best of the weather and is easily accessible by the A832 either from Dundonnell in the north or Aultbea in the south.

A car park is conveniently situated behind sand dunes near the bridge over the Inverianvie river, one of two rushing streams which enter the bay from the south.

If you walk north along the shore for half-a-mile you arrive at a charming and secluded horseshoe bay enclosed by the arms of two tidal islands. Many are the times that I have fished for mackerel off the end of these islands while my children have swum in the shallow water or collected shells. Gruinard Bay can be idyllic at any time of the year; the gulf stream has made swimming possible even on sunny days in March, provided we have lit a roaring driftwood fire for a warm up afterwards.

On several occasions we have seen divers and schools of cavorting harbour porpoises in the bay. Golden eagles have soared overhead and wild goats have grazed nearby.

A mile off shore stands Gruinard Island of sinister renown but now free of anthrax after 45 years. During the last war the island was used to test the effectiveness on sheep of bombs containing anthrax spores. The sheep died quickly but the island was seriously contaminated and warning notices were hastily erected. After twenty years the concentration of the spores had not decreased.

Eventually in 1985 the soil was treated with a mixture of formaldehyde and sea water which proved very effective at killing the spores. By October 1987 the island was declared free of danger and forty non-breeding Cheviot ewes were allowed to graze. They suffered no ill effects and this unsavoury chapter in the history of this most attractive Scottish island is now closed.

Corrieshalloch Gorge

From the road junction at Braemore, the Abhainn Droma cascades steeply down to Strath More, where it becomes the river Broom, through the mile long, deep and narrow Corrieshalloch Gorge.

For a distance of 150ft the water plunges over a black and glistening rock step, while the sides of the ravine are clad in ferns, mosses, rhododendrons, pines and a wide variety of broad leaved trees. These are the renowned Falls of Measach which are owned by the National Trust for Scotland.

A car park and toilet block are situated on the other side of the A835 to the falls. Access is through a gate to a steep little path leading to a suspension bridge which spans the falls. This splendid bridge which takes you dizzily across the gorge, 200ft above the river, was built by Sir John Fowler who designed the Forth railway bridge.

Inverlael Forest Trail

The Lael Forest on the east side of the A835 clothes the lower slopes of the Beinn Dearg range. Various waymarked walks can be enjoyed here, both through the forest itself and through a forest garden of interesting trees from home and abroad.

There are giant redwoods and cedars, silver firs and whitebeams. The flora is rich, the bird life varied and the trails give enticing views of the Fannichs.

As you drive alongside the forest between the end of Loch Broom and Braemore Junction you will see the Forest Trail car park and picnic site.

Leckmelm Gardens

These gardens, which are open every day from April to September are situated three miles south of Ullapool between the A835 and Loch Broom. The ten acre arboretum and two-and-a-half acre walled garden was laid out in 1870. It lay unattended for forty five years until restoration began in 1985. It contains many splendid and rare trees and a wide range of species and hybrid rhododendrons, azaleas and other shrubs.

Ullapool

The largest village in Wester Ross with a wide range of facilities including sports centre, swimming bath, climbing wall, tennis, pony trekking, fishing trips, pleasure cruises, mountain bike hire, Land Rover safaris, excellent shops and two museums.

Ullapool was created by the British Fishery Society in 1788 and it is now an important fishing port and car ferry link to Stornoway on the Isle of Lewis.

The Summer Isles

The cluster of islands in the mouth of Loch Broom are called the Summer Isles. This is a seemingly appropriate name when the islands are bathed in sunshine while the clouds are down on the mainland mountains.

The Isles are seen particularly clearly, dotted on the blue ocean, from Beinn Ghobhlach and the Fiddler of Ben Mor Coigach or from the roadside at Achiltibuie and Mellon Udrigle.

Many years ago we camped as a family on Priest Island for several idyllic days. This is the remotest of the Summer Isles and we were delivered and taken off by fishing boat. Nowadays visitors are not allowed on the island which is an RSPB bird sanctuary.

Years later we enjoyed another memorable camp on Tanera Beg which is easily accessible from Badentarbat. The large, adjacent, Tanera Mor is the only island with a permanent settlement, although there is a holiday house on Eilean Dubh. In 1783 a herring-curing industry was established on Tanera Mor employing over a hundred people. Today there is a small cafe and a post office which sells Commemorative Summer Isles stamps.

St Martin's Isle is situated just off Ardmair Bay and contains the remains of a chapel, several carved headstones and an unusual cross with double arms. It is not known whether the island was named after St Martin of Iona or after a St Martin who built the chapel.

The Summer Isles are wonderful places to see a myriad sea birds, both Atlantic grey and common seals and (possibly) cetaceans. Several boats operate out of Ullapool offering a variety of cruises: fishing trips, sunset cruises, wildlife cruises, cruises to Tanera Mor for tea and cruises to Carn nan Sgeir (one of the nearest islands) for a picnic. Summer Isles cruises also operate out of Badentarbat near Achiltibuie.

By far the best accounts of the Summer Isles are to be found in the books *Island Years* and *Island Farm* by the naturalist Fraser Darling. He lived on Priest Island and crofted on Tanera Mor for several years in the 1930s and 1940s and he writes with great affection and authority on the natural history of these islands.

Achiltibuie

A sprawling village of whitewashed cottages opposite the Summer Isles and under Ben Mor Coigach.

A remarkable hydroponicum has been built by Robert Irvine. This harnesses heat and sunlight in a double skinned greenhouse and allows many exotic fruits and flowers to be grown, with the plants obtaining nutrients solely from the natural local water. The hydroponicum is open to visitors between Easter and October.

Summer Isles Foods, Achiltibuie, sell smoked delicacies to the public during the summer months.

Knockan Cliff

Knockan cliff overlooks the A835 just south of Elphin and is an extension of the Inverpolly Nature Reserve. There is a small visitor's centre and a geological trail which winds up the cliff.

In 1859 Professor Nicol, studying the sequence of different rocks at Knockan, put forward his hypothesis that faulting had forced older highly altered schists on top of the more recent Durness limestone. This became known as the Moine Thrust.

The geological trail and its accompanying leaflet explain clearly, and in layman's terms, the unique rock strata at Knockan.

Elphin

Highland and Rare Breeds Farm with over thirty breeds to see over fifteen acres. Open every day May-September.

Caves of the Assynt Area

The Cambrian limestone, which outcrops in many places in Assynt, has been worn away by the dissolving action of the carbonic acid in rain water over many thousands of years. This has produced caves and tunnels in the rock and three sites are of special interest. They all involve short walks from the road and make ideal expeditions even for non-speleologists.

Some of these caves have rivers roaring into them, some are near dry stream beds and some are half way up cliff faces, but all are surrounded by limestone outcrops, thick grass and a rich flora.

Do not venture far into these caves without the proper equipment and an expert on hand. Serious speleologists will find the book *The Caves of Assynt*, published by the Grampian Speleological Group, very informative.

The Uamh an Tartair Cave

This cave lies on the Abhainn a'Chnocain. It is marked Uamh an Tartair on the map (217091) and can be approached using a hill track running south from the hamlet of Knockan near Elphin.

From Knockan pass through a gate onto a rough track which leads in a mile to the dry river bed of the Abhainn a'Chnocain. A short way up the river bed you reach a low, wet limestone cliff which can be easily climbed on either side.

Above the cliff the rushing river is met once more, disappearing down a swallow hole into the depths of the hillside, while another low cliff hung with mountain ash trees surrounds the grotto.

This is a lovely spot (and a fine place for a picnic) with cropped green grass and white boulders of Durness limestone. It looks out north to the massif of Breabag, Conival and Ben More Assynt.

The Caves of Allt nan Uamh

This is a short but fascinating expedition to a series of caves in a limestone crag on the west side of the quartzite ridge of Breabag. The caves, which lie within the Inchnadamph NNR were investigated in 1917 by Peach and Horne and found to contain two human skeletons dating from 6,000 BC and bones of animals such as lynx, bear and reindeer long extinct in Britain.

Park near the bridge (253179) where there is a large fish hatchery in green corrugated iron sheds, not marked on the map. A narrow path runs up on the north side of the tumbling Allt nan Uamh which can soon be seen welling up from a spring in the hillside itself. Continue to follow the dry river bed for one kilometre until an impressive limestone cliff can be seen on the south side.

Scramble up limestone scree and grass to investigate a succession of caves beneath the overhanging brow of the cliff. Narrow passages can be seen disappearing into the bowels of the earth but there are no easily entered inner chambers as in the nearby Gleann Dubh caves. This is a wild and rocky corrie and it is easy to imagine these caves being the lair of man or beast when the ice was retreating from the Highlands only 10,000 years ago.

Beyond the line of caves the river forks, and the northerly branch includes a fine limestone ravine with more caves, waterfalls and a rich and varied flora.

The Grampian Speleological Group are very active in this area and have explored over 1300 metres of passages to date.

The Caves of Gleann Dubh near Inchnadamph

From Inchnadamph walk up the path beside the Traligill river for about a mile until the river can be seen to emerge from beneath a low crag. In dry weather the passage can be explored for some distance until the roof descends to water level.

Further up the glen, above the south side of the river, lie three more caves. These can be entered and several inner chambers explored with a torch, provided that sensible safety precautions are taken.

Once again the GSG are active here and have penetrated over 150m into some of the caves.

Ardvreck Castle

Nobody who drives up the A837 north of Inchnadamph can fail to be impressed by the gaunt ruined castle of Ardvreck. It stands on a spit of land jutting out into Loch Assynt with waves lapping almost to the walls themselves, and when it is silhouetted against the setting sun with the surrounding mountains mirrored in the loch it becomes, for me, the ultimate romantic Highland castle.

Cars may be parked in a layby whence a short stroll across cropped grass brings you to the castle. You may wander round and explore the keep and dungeons at will. There is no charge.

Ardvreck Castle was built in 1597 as the seat of MacLeod of Assynt and it was there that in 1650 the fugitive Montrose, who had been fighting the royalist cause for Charles II, came to seek refuge. But Neil MacLeod, the eleventh chief of Assynt, cast Montrose into his dungeons and claimed the £20,000 reward. Montrose was later taken to Edinburgh and executed.

However, soon after this event, MacLeod himself was forced to flee as MacKenzie, Earl of Seaforth, seized Assynt and held it for a hundred years.

The shell-like ruin which still stands just south of Ardvreck Castle is Eddrachalder or Calda House. This mansion house was built about 1660 by MacKenzie the new owner of Assynt.

Kirkaig Falls 4 miles/6km

The short but tumultuous river Kirkaig drains the vast catchment area south of Suilven which contains an interlinked system of lochs: the Cam Loch, Loch Veyatie and the Fionn Loch.

The Kirkaig Falls lie about two miles upstream from the road bridge near Loch Kirkaig and are well worth a visit, particularly after rain when the water thunders down a black cliff in a welter of spray, while rainbows arch over the deep pool below.

Parking is available near the bridge and the path starts from behind the remote but extremely well stocked bookshop of Achins. It keeps to the riverside where you can see, at regular intervals, stone piers built for fishermen because the Kirkaig is a noted salmon river.

The banks are well wooded and where the river disappears into a gorge the path climbs above the trees traversing the bare hillside. Although the path continues to the Fionn Loch, and provides a useful approach to Suilven, a large cairn marks the place where you should turn off and descend to the river at the Kirkaig Falls. The roar of the water can be easily heard and, standing on a rock ledge overlooking the pool, you may see salmon leaping and flashing in vain attempts to surmount the falls.

Unless you are planning to continue walking to Suilven there is no alternative but to retrace your steps to the road.

Lochinver

A thriving white-fish port and holiday centre with a range of shops, boat trips and a large stoneware workshop which is open on weekdays throughout the year.

The new roads, quay and sheds are part of a multi-million pound development funded largely by the EEC.

Eas a'Chual Aluinn Falls

Loch Glencoul and Loch Beag run inland from Kylesku into the very wild tract of mountainous country north of Ben More Assynt and typified by the rock castle known as the Stack of Glencoul.

Just beyond the head of Loch Beag an amazing waterfall plunges over the cliffs of Leitir Dhubh to the glen far below. At over 600ft the falls, known as Eas a'Chual Aluinn or The Maiden's Tresses, are the highest in Britain and nearly four times the height of Niagara.

However, the cliff is not sheer and the water bounds down in two main leaps. The falls are tucked away out of sight of the nearest road and, if you make an expedition to see them, it is best to come after rain for in dry weather the volume of water is slight and you may be disappointed.

Boat trips up Loch Glencoul and Loch Beag from Kylesku to near the foot of the falls are run daily in the summer season, but you still cannot see the full extent of the falls from the boat. A popular walk in from the south to the top of the falls takes the well cairned path leaving the A894 at Loch na Gainmhich, climbs to Loch Bealach a'Bhurich and then follows the stream to the lip of the falls. From here it is possible to peer over the edge and view the top section of the falls but the ground is steep and treacherous and care is needed.

The best way to see the falls in all their glory is to walk in from Unapool or Kylestrome alongside Lochs Glencoul or Glendhu as described in the chapter on the ascent of the Stack of Glencoul.

It is extraordinary that on the north side of the glen, directly opposite Eas a'Chual Aluinn, another spectacular cascade foams down the cliffs and is barely overshadowed by its more illustrious neighbour.

Note: In 1984 a tragic accident occurred in strange circumstances at Eas a'Chual Aluinn. The wife of an insurance broker was killed when she stumbled and fell over the falls. At the inquest the broker, Malcolm Hussey, admitted that he might have knocked against her accidentally causing her to slip out of sight.

It was revealed that Mr Hussey had recently doubled the insurance on their death to £100,000. The police inspector asked Mr Hussey if he had read a newspaper article dated the day before the accident about a Dutchman who had been convicted of murder after throwing his wife over Salisbury Crags in Edinburgh but Mr Hussey denied this.

The inquest returned a verdict of accidental death.

Two years later there was a final twist to the tragic event when Mr Hussey was found dead in his fume-filled car.

Fanagmore
A tiny village north of Tarbet (the Handa Island ferry terminal) where boat trips to see seals and birds in Loch Laxford can be obtained.

Kinlochbervie
A fishing port in north-west Sutherland used by about thirty boats. It has an ice plant and fish auctions are held several times a week. There are shops, restaurants, a hotel and the usual facilities including sea angling and bird watching trips.

Durness
Durness is Britain's most north-westerly settlement. It has a nine hole golf course and several excellent beaches.

Balnakeil Craft Village just outside Durness has been established in once-derelict buildings which were owned by the Ministry of Defence. You can watch potters, weavers, printers, jewellers and workers in enamel, horn, wood and leather.

Smoo Cave
Situated just east of Durness this is Britain's largest limestone sea cave. You can explore it on foot from below, peer into it through blowholes from above or take boat tours into its innermost recesses.

Loch Eriboll
Choraidh Croft Farm exhibits rare breeds and has a museum of crofting life, a marine life building, pets corner and cafe. The farm is situated half way down the west side of Loch Eriboll.

APPENDIX

Tourist Information Centres
North Kessock 01463 731505
Gairloch 01445 712130
Ullapool 01854 612135
Dornoch 01862 810400
Lochinver 01571 844330
Durness 01971 511259

National Trust for Scotland
Information Centre Torridon 01445 791221

Scottish Natural Heritage
Inverness 01463 239431

Scotrail
0345 550033

Highland Scottish Omnibus Company
Inverness 01463 233371

Mountain Weather Forecasts
North West Scotland Mountain Forecast: 0891 500441
Western Highlands Five Day Forecast: 0336 444900

The Falls of Measach and Corrieshalloch Gorge, a National Trust for Scotland property near Ullapool. Photo: Tom Rix.

BIBLIOGRAPHY

The Munros Scottish Mountaineering Club Hillwalkers' Guide Vol. 1 by D. Bennet.

200 Challenging Walks in Britain and Ireland by Richard Gilbert, Diadem.

The High Mountains of Britain and Ireland by Irvine Butterfield, Diadem.

The North West Highlands District Guide by D. Bennet and T. Strang, Scottish Mountaineering Club.

The Corbetts and Other Scottish Hills Scottish Mountaineering Club Hillwalkers' Guide Vol. 2 by S. Johnstone, H. Brown and D. Bennett.

Climbing The Corbetts by Hamish Brown, Gollancz.

On Hills Of The North by J. Hubert Walker, Oliver and Boyd, 1948.

Short Walks Around Gairloch by Steve Chadwick, and *Poolewe to Guinard, Selected Walks and Caves* by Steve Chadwick, Private Publications.

INDEX

Rear cover: Slioch seen from the woods of Caledonian pine on the south side of Loch Maree. Photo: Ian Evans.